COUNTDOWN TO DOOMSDAY

First published in 2020 by
New Life Publishing, Luton
Bedfordshire LU4 9HG

© Pat Collins C.M. 2020

British Library Cataloguing in Publication Data
A catalogue record for this book is available
from the British Library

ISBN 978 1 912237 20 3

Typesetting by Goodnews Books,
Luton, UK www.goodnewsbooks..co.uk
Printed and bound in Great Britain

COUNTDOWN TO DOOMSDAY

HOW OUR WORLD WILL END

'Men of Galilee,' they said, 'why do you stand here
looking into the sky? This same Jesus,
who has been taken from you into heaven,
will come back in the same way you have
seen him go into heaven' (Acts 1:11)

PAT COLLINS C.M.

Dedicated with gratitude to Paolo Pancaldi
who, for the last quarter of a century,
has been my faithful collaborator,
companion and interpreter
during my many visits to Italy

Eileen (Bridget) Mc Cormack
Knockgreana, Old Pallas
Co. Limerick

CONTENTS

PREFACE

WRITING ANY BOOK IS DIFFICULT because it requires a lot of thought, concentration and effort. However, if one is writing on a subject with which one is familiar it is not so difficult because there is not a need to do a lot of new reading and reflection. I must admit, that I have found that Countdown to Doomsday, has proven to be the most difficult book I have written to date and I have wondered why this was so.

Over a period of time I began to realise that in spite of the fact that I have a number of degrees in theology, I had heard very little about Christ's second coming either during my college years or subsequently. As a result I had to do an unusual amount of reading in preparation for writing this book. Furthermore, the more I reflected on the subject of eschatology, the more my former ways of thinking were challenged and changed. I found myself going through a painful intellectual conversion, one in which the end times, slowly but surely, became a new focal point of all my theology and spirituality. As a result I began to reinterpret the Church's teaching about the coming of the kingdom of God in the light of the four last things. I came to see that in the incarnation of Jesus, his public ministry, especially his healings, miracles, exorcisms and resurrection, not only was heaven touching earth, there were intimations of the advent of a new heaven and a new earth to come. That is what we ask for when we say in the Lord's

Prayer, 'your kingdom come, your will be done, on earth as it is in heaven'(Mt 6:10).

Jesus promised all those who believed in him, 'Very truly I tell you, whoever believes in me will do the works I have been doing, and they will do even greater things than these, because I am going to the Father' (Jn 14:12). Speaking about the implications of that verse par 452 of the Catechism of the Catholic Church explains, 'Christ enables us to live in him all that he himself lived, and he lives it in us. By his Incarnation, He, the Son of God, has in a certain way united himself with each person. We are called only to become one with him, for he enables us as the members of his Body to share in what he lived for us in his flesh as our model: We must continue to accomplish in ourselves the stages of Jesus' life and his mysteries.' So, whenever, we Christians live and minister in the power of the Holy Spirit, while exercising the charisms, especially those of power (cf. 1 Cor 12:8-10) we are not only manifesting the coming of the kingdom of God, we are manifesting something of what is to come, in all its wonderful fullness, at the end of time.

I suspect that many readers may find that this is a difficult book to read not only because of the unfamiliar and at times technical content, but also because of my deficiencies as an author. Nevertheless I'd encourage you to work your way through it because I think that like me, you will find the teachings of the scriptures and the Church will be rewarding as you grasp their meaning and exciting implications.

I want to take this opportunity to thank Gerard and Toni Pomfret of New Life Publishing for all their help in publishing this, the third volume in a trilogy of books.

INTRODUCTION

I N 1947 MEMBERS OF THE *BULLETIN OF ATOMIC SCIENTISTS* introduced the notion of the doomsday[1] clock. It was intended to represent the possibility of a global catastrophe occurring at 'midnight' on a clock whose twenty four hours represented human history. Each year since 1947 the *Bulletin* has weighed up the main threats to human life, and indicated the danger level by saying how many minutes and / or seconds we are from midnight. For example, in 1947 they said it was seven minutes. In 2019, they said it was only two minutes! The principal factors influencing the doomsday clock are such things as the possibility of nuclear conflict and catastrophic climate change.

In this connection it is worth noting that many scholars are currently investigating what is known as existential risk. The term refers to catastrophic danger where an adverse outcome would either annihilate intelligent life or permanently and drastically curtail its potential. For instance, The Cambridge University Project for Existential Risk states that the 'greatest threats' to the human species are man-made, namely, artificial intelligence, global warming, nuclear war, and rogue biotechnology, e.g. a deadly man made virus. One of its founders, Prof Martin Rees gave an

---

[1] The Oxford English Dictionary says that the word 'doomsday' refers to, 'a day of judgement or trial, when sentence is pronounced. Also, a day of final dissolution, as at the end of the world.'

interesting Ted Talk entitled, *'Can we prevent the end of the world?'*[2]
The Future of Humanity Institute in Oxford University also states
that human extinction is more likely to result from human causes
than natural ones. These groups estimate that the risk of
humankind becoming extinct during the next 100 years is 9.5%.

In 1954 I was nine years of age. At that time my father, a veterinary
surgeon, was working in a government laboratory. He used to cycle
there and back each day. On one occasion, when he returned home,
he said that he had met a beggar who had told him that the end of
the world was going to occur on the 8th of December that year. I
didn't quite know what to expect. But on Dec 8th Dublin was
deluged with the worst rainfall in 100 years. Instead of water going
down the shores it was gushing out of them. During the day the
whole area where we lived was flooded. Our back garden filled
with water. Although our house was elevated quite a few feet above
the ground the waters kept on rising until they were nearly coming
into the house. A few miles away, the water level in the river Tolka
had risen to an unprecedented height of nearly twenty feet and the
railway bridge had fallen into the raging torrent. For a time I felt
that the poor man who had spoken to my father about the world's
end occurring on the feast of the Immaculate Conception, might
well have been correct. But then the rains stopped and the waters
slowly receded. When we re-emerged from our house we found
that the whole district was littered with flotsam and jetsam such as
apples, pieces of wood, paper and sacks, much of which had floated
out of people's garden sheds. That was my first experience of an
apocalyptic prediction.

A few years later, when I was seventeen the Cuban missile crisis

[2] https://www.youtube.com/watch?v=tMSU6k5-WXg

took place over a period of thirteen days in October 1962. President Kennedy of America warned chairman Khrushchev of the Soviet Union that if his ships, which were carrying missiles for placement in Cuba, didn't turn back there could be a nuclear war. I can remember how on Oct 27th when the crisis was reaching its climax I went to school with a small transistor radio which I listened to at every possible opportunity. I was anxious to get the news of what was happening. Like my fellow pupils I thought that it might be our last day at school if war broke out and nuclear weapons were used. I can recall that on my way home from school I called into my local church and prayed fervently. I asked God not to let nuclear war occur. My prayers, as well as those of millions of others, were heard when the next morning, October 28th the Soviet ships turned back and premier Khrushchev issued a public statement which said that Soviet missiles would be dismantled and removed from Cuba.

After that, I cannot say that I gave much thought to the end of the world until I was a young adult. When I studied theology I became aware that the Bible talks about two advents of Christ. The Old Testament was punctuated for nearly a thousand years with messianic promises that anticipated the coming of the suffering servant mentioned by Isaiah. Those promises were finally fulfilled when Jesus was born two thousand years ago. Scripture scholars maintain that he was an eschatological prophet, someone who looked forward to the in-breaking of the reign of God which would occur in a definitive way in the end times when Jesus would come again as triumphant king.

Following the ascension of Jesus the first believers waited for his second coming at an indeterminate time in the future. In the early Church they expressed their longing for Christ's return by praying,

'*Maranatha*'. This Aramaic word can be translated as, 'O Lord, come!' It is worth pointing out, that this understanding is supported by what appears to be a Greek equivalent in Rev 22:20, where it says, 'Amen. Come, Lord Jesus!' Echoing the teaching of Jesus himself about the end times, par. 39 of *The Pastoral Constitution Gaudium et Spes* (The Church in the Modern World) says, 'We do not know the time of the consummation of the earth and humanity . . . On this earth the kingdom is already present in mystery. When the Lord returns, it will be brought into full flower.'

I can remember that during my student days we used the technical phrase, 'realised eschatology' to describe the fact that the kingdom of God is already present in a nascent way, but will only come to full fruition in the second coming of Jesus. An even more obscure technical way of expressing the *already* and *not yet* nature of the reign of God was to say that the second coming of Christ is proleptically present, i.e., it is already partially present. As I have reflected on the subject of apocalyptic prophecy I have increasingly come to see that all the factors we associate with the end times, such as tribulation, wars, upheavals in nature, apostasy, and the activity of the Antichrist, are already present in an anticipatory way in every era of human history and, as such, are intimations, in the present, of events which will reach a crescendo just before the second coming of Jesus. They are like the overture to an opera which gives a hint of what is later to be enacted in a more fully realised and developed way.

MY CHANGING ATTITUDE TO THE SECOND COMING

When I studied the New Testament during my seminary years I got the impression that both Jesus, St Paul, and members of the early Church expected that the end of the world would occur within a relatively short period of time. For example, in 1 Thess 4:13-18, which was written around 52 A.D., Paul wrote,

> 'We would not have you ignorant, brethren, concerning those who are asleep, that you may not grieve as others do who have no hope. For since we believe that Jesus died and rose again, even so, through Jesus, God will bring with him those who have fallen asleep. For this we declare to you by the word of the Lord, that *we who are alive, who are left until the coming of the Lord,* shall not precede those who have fallen asleep. For the Lord himself will descend from heaven with a cry of command, with the archangel's call, and with the sound of the trumpet of God. And the dead in Christ will rise first; then we who are alive, who are left, shall be caught up together with them in the clouds to meet the Lord in the air; and so we shall always be with the Lord. Therefore comfort one another with these words.'

That passage seemed to suggest that Christ's second coming would take place during the lifetime of some of Paul's fellow Christians, but when that expectation was not fulfilled, perhaps St Paul began to think that Christ's second coming would be delayed for an indefinite period of time. In any case, speaking about the end times Jesus himself had admitted, 'about that day or hour no one knows, not even the angels in heaven, nor the Son, but only the Father' (Mt 24:26). Furthermore, I knew that over the centuries there had been many people, including some saints, who had confidently predicted the immanence of the end-times only to be proven to be mistaken, time and time again. So, like many others I came to the conclusion that although the second coming would be significant for those who would be living when it occurred, it wasn't likely to occur any time soon, so there wasn't much point in focusing on it. In more recent years, however, my attitude to Christ's second coming has changed quite a bit for three main reasons. To begin, I am growing old. As my natural life nears its end I'm more focused on eschatology, what the Church refers to as the four last things, death, judgement, heaven, and hell. Furthermore, over a period of time I have come to increasingly appreciate that Jesus was an eschatological prophet with an apocalyptic message. For instance, eminent Protestant theologian Karl Barth wrote, 'Christianity that is not entirely and altogether eschatology has entirely nothing to do with Christ.'[3] Another respected Protestant theologian, Jurgen Moltmann, wrote in similar vein when he stated, 'The eschatological is not one element of Christianity, but it is the medium of Christian faith... Hence eschatology cannot really be only part of Christian doctrine. Rather, the eschatological outlook is characteristic of all Christian proclamation, of every existence and of the whole Church.'[4] Joseph Ratzinger, who later became Pope Benedict XVI, said in his *Eschatology: Death and Eternal Life*, 'Eschatology has moved to the very centre of the theological stage. Some twenty years ago Hans von Balthasar called it the 'storm zone' of contemporary theology.'[5] Finally, eminent Catholic scripture scholar John P Meier says, 'Jesus not only presented himself as the eschatological prophet of the coming kingdom of God, not only presented himself as the Elijah-like miracle-worker who made the future kingdom already effective and palpable to his followers, but at the same time presented himself as a teacher who could tell Israelites how to observe the Law of Moses - indeed, who

---

[3] The Epistle to the Romans (London: Oxford University Press, 1933), 314.

[4] The Theology of Hope (London: SCM Press, 1967), 16.

[5] (Washington: Washington University Press, 1988), 1.

could even tell Israelites what they should or should not observe in the Law.'[6]

Finally, in recent years I have written two interrelated books. In 2015 I published, *Guided by God: Ordinary and Charismatic Ways of Discovering God's will*. It asserted that a supernatural realm exists and that God can communicate with believers by revealing the divine presence, word and will to those who are open to God's self-communication in the Holy Spirit. While I was reflecting on the nature and types of divine revelation, I became very interested in the subject of prophecy as the premier charism which has enabled men and women down the ages to receive messages from God which surpass the ability of the unaided, natural mind. As a result I wrote, *Prophecy: Truth for Today Light for Tomorrow,* which was published in 2018. Apparently, 27% of the Bible is devoted to prophecy. It is estimated that it contains over two thousand prophetic messages. Unlike vague, non-biblical forecasts, such as those to be found in the Mayan prophecy and the writings of Nostradamus and St Malachy, those in the Bible are specific and correct. For example, when Tyre was at the height of its power, sometime between 593–571 BC, the prophet Ezekiel predicted its total destruction.

'They will destroy the walls of Tyre and pull down her towers; I will scrape away her rubble and make her a bare rock. . . They will plunder your wealth and loot your merchandise; they will break down your walls and demolish your fine houses and throw your stones, timber and rubble into the sea. . . I will make you a bare rock, and you will

---

[6] *A Marginal Jew: Rethinking the Historical Jesus,* Volume 2 (New York: Doubleday 1994), 1046.

become a place to spread fishnets. You will never be rebuilt, for I the LORD have spoken, declares the Sovereign LORD.' (Ezech 26:4,12,14).

While the destruction of the city could have been plausible, the prophecy that it would be thrown into the midst of the sea, and its former location be scraped like the top of a rock, seemed to be utterly implausible. Yet both these prophecies were fulfilled. Around 570 BC Nebuchadnezzar besieged the city for years and conquered it. The inhabitants of Tyre, however, escaped to a nearby island where they inhabited another city. Meantime, Nebuchadnezzar reduced their former city to rubble. Two and a half centuries later Alexander the Great attacked the island city of Tyre. He ordered his troops to build a causeway to the island by piling the ancient ruins of mainland Tyre into the sea, thus fulfilling the prophecy that Tyre would be thrown into the midst of the sea. Tyre was conquered and most of its inhabitants slaughtered. As Is 46:9-10 attests, 'I am God, and there is none like me, declaring the end from the beginning and from ancient times things not yet done, saying, My counsel shall stand, and I will accomplish all my purpose.' In other words, we can rely with confidence on the prophetic word of God.

The many Old Testament prophecies to do with the first coming of Christ as the suffering servant who was a descendant of king David, were fulfilled in remarkable detail in the course of the life, death and resurrection of Jesus. In this book we will focus on apocalyptic prophecies which speak about Christ's second coming as victorious king at the end of the world. Those prophecies predict that before the end comes certain marker events will take place. Needless to say, we will focus on them later in this book. Two very popular DVDs entitled, *The Final Prophecies* and *The Coming Convergence* suggest that the end times may occur in the relatively near rather than the distant future. Their large sales indicate that many people, both religious and secular are interested in the subject.[7] As a result many people have come to the conclusion that although, strictly speaking, we have been living in the end times ever since the resurrection and ascension of Jesus, there is reason to believe that currently we may be living during the final run-in period before Christ comes again.

A good deal of this book will be devoted to exploring arguments for and against this point of view. Meantime, the personal lives of all of us mirror what is going to take place on a universal scale. As Ps 39:4 says, 'show me, Lord, my life's end and the number of my days; let me know how fleeting my life is.' Our personal end, like that of history, will occur at an indefinite time in the future. It seems prudent, therefore, that our Christian lives should be lived in the lively expectation of what is yet to come. As Jesus said at the end of the parable of the wise and unwise virgins, 'Watch therefore, for you don't know the day nor the hour in which the Son of Man is coming' (Mt 25:13).

PLAN AND APPROACH OF THE BOOK
Broadly speaking, this book will deal with a number of topics.

- Firstly, in Amos 3:7 we read, 'For the Lord God does nothing without revealing his secret to his servants the prophets.' That being so we will look at relevant passages in the Old and New Testaments which refer, in one way or another, to the end times. Relying on the research of reputable scripture scholars we will

[7] Ingenuity Films.

try to discover what the inspired word of God has to say about the second coming of Jesus.

• Secondly, we will look at what the *magisterium* of the Catholic Church has taught in an official way down the centuries. As Pope Francis said in par. 173 of *Evangelium Gaudium* (Rejoice and be Glad), 'listening entails obedience to the Gospel as the ultimate standard, but also to the Magisterium that guards it, as we seek to find in the treasury of the Church whatever is most fruitful for the 'today' of salvation.'

• Thirdly, we will look at what the fathers and doctors of the Church have reliably taught on this subject. Writing about their authority, Pope Leo XIII said in par. 30 of his Encyclical *Providentissimus Deus* (On the Study of Holy Scripture), 'The Holy Fathers are of supreme authority whenever they all interpret in one and the same manner any text of the Bible . . . for their unanimity clearly evinces that such interpretation has come down from the Apostles as a matter of Catholic faith.'

• Fourthly, to a limited extent, we will listen to what some saints, visionaries and prophets, whose private revelations have been approved by the Church, have had to say about the end times.[8]

• Fifthly, we will look at a series of significant marker events that have been mentioned in a prophetic way in the Bible and foretell the events that will precede the second coming of the Lord. This book will seek to answer an all important question. Although we cannot know exactly when the second coming of Jesus will occur, do those marker events give us an indication that the end times might be approaching in the near future?

• Sixthly, we will look briefly at some of the spiritual implications of Christian eschatology at this critical time in the life of the people of God.

---

[8] Cf. Pat Collins, C.M., 'Private Revelation,' in *Guided by God* (Luton: New Life Publishing, 2015), 189-209.

Happily there are a large number of books available on the various topics we will be examining. I have recommended some of them in the bibliography. There is a Latin saying, which is often quoted by Catholics, namely, *virtus in medio stat*, i.e., virtue stands in the middle. As far as methodology is concerned, I want to steer a course between a fundamentalist and a liberal approach.

A fundamentalist is someone who interprets the scriptures in a literal manner, without the aid of textual or historical criticism. St Paul VI said in his *Credo* (The Creed of the People of God), 'The intellect which God has given us reaches *that which is*, and not merely the subjective expression of the structures and development of consciousness; and, on the other hand, that the task of interpretation – of hermeneutics – is to try to understand and extricate, while respecting the word expressed, the sense conveyed by a text, and not to recreate, in some fashion, this sense in accordance with arbitrary hypotheses.'[9] Speaking about scriptural interpretation of the proper kind St John Paul II said, 'Attention must be given to the literary forms of the various biblical books in order to determine the intentions of the sacred writers. And it is most helpful, at times crucial, to be aware of the personal situation of the biblical writer, of the circumstances of culture, time, language, etc., which influenced the way the message was presented... In this way, it is possible to avoid a narrow fundamentalism which distorts the whole truth.'[10] While that point is true for all scriptural interpretation, it is especially true when it comes to interpreting apocalyptic writings which are composed in a characteristically symbolic way.

---

[9] (London: Catholic Truth Society, 1968), 4-5.

[10] Address of John Paul II to the executive committee of the world Catholic Federation for the Biblical apostolate April 7th 1986, par. 3.

Liberal theology, on the other hand, tends on *a priori* grounds, which had their origins in the Enlightenment, to strip out all the supernatural aspects of the scriptures. As Pope Benedict said in his apostolic exhortation *Verbum Domini* (The Word of God in the Life and Mission of the Church) par. 35 B, 'The lack of a hermeneutic of faith with regard to Scripture entails more than a simple absence; in its place there inevitably enters another hermeneutic, a positivistic and *secularised hermeneutic* ultimately based on the conviction that the Divine does not intervene in human history. According to this hermeneutic, whenever a divine element seems present, it has to be explained in some other way, reducing everything to the human element. This leads to interpretations that deny the historicity of the divine elements.' For example, well known Protestant scripture scholar Rudolf Bultmann wrote, 'The historical method includes the presupposition that history is a unity in the sense of a closed continuum of effects in which individual events are connected by the succession of cause and effect....This closedness means that the continuum of historical happenings *cannot be rent by the interference of supernatural transcendent powers and that therefore there is no 'miracle'* in this sense of the word.'[11]

While I do think that it is true to say that there are mythological elements in Biblical apocalyptic, the notion of myth should not be understood as being synonymous with falsehood. In a note at the beginning of his book *The Jesus Myth*, Andrew Greeley wrote, 'A

---

[11] 'Exegesis without Presuppositions' in *Existence and Faith* (Meridian Books, 1960), 291-292. See also interesting things that Pope Benedict XVI had to say about orthodox scripture interpretation both in the introduction to his trilogy *Jesus of Nazareth* and in par. 35 of his post-synodal, apostolic declaration *Verbum Domini* (The Word of the Lord).

myth is a symbolic story which demonstrates in Allan Watt's words, 'the inner meaning of the universe and of human life.' . . . Or as A.K. Coomaraswamy observes, 'Myth embodies the nearest approach to absolute truth that can be stated in words.'[12]

Although many writers of the calibre of Sts Robert Bellarmine, and John Henry Newman had a great and inspired knowledge of the scriptures they did not interpret them either with the aid of the modern historical, critical method, nor form, source or redaction criticism. Instead they were inclined to support their understanding of individual texts in a traditional manner. Firstly, they did so by adverting to the literal and the spiritual meaning of the writings, the latter being subdivided into the allegorical, moral and anagogical senses.[13] The anagogical sense of scripture, is particularly relevant in the context of this book because it refers to the interpretation of texts which relate to the end of time, when the kingdom of God will be finally and definitively established. Those who espoused the traditional understanding of scripture would often support their exegesis by citing the authoritative interpretations of the Fathers and Doctors of the Church. With these methodological points in mind I hope to employ a more contemporary approach in order to arrive at a sense of what is true about the end times as revealed by God.

I should say at the outset that I am very committed to ecumenism. However, as far as the subject of eschatology is concerned I feel that some evangelical and Pentecostal Protestants have developed very questionable forms of apocalyptic interpretation, for example

---

12 (London: Search Press, 1972), 11.

13 'The Senses of Scripture,' in *Catechism of the Catholic Church*, pars. 113-19.

their interrelated notions of dispensationalism[14] and the rapture. While I will mention their views in passing, I will not focus on them. For a critique of those misguided approaches see Terry Frazier's, *A Second Look at the Second Coming: Sorting through the Speculations.*[15] For my part, I will focus on what the Catholic Church and many mainline Protestants teach about the End times.

CONCLUSION

When I started to read and reflect on the topic of apocalyptic prophecy I came to appreciate, in a way that I had failed to do heretofore, what a large, detailed and complex subject it really is. I am painfully aware that this particular study of the subject is far from comprehensive. Instead of looking carefully at all the relevant texts in the Old and New Testaments about the end times, I have restricted myself to those that I think are of particular interest. Added to that, I have deliberately avoided conducting a detailed account of topics such as, futurist, historicist, idealist and preterist views of the end times, as well as scriptural topics such as the whore of Babylon (Rev 17:5), the mark of the beast (Rev 13:16) and the significance of the fifth bowl (Rev 16:10-11). Furthermore as Desmond A Birch's long book. *Trial, Tribulation & Triumph: Before, During, and After Antichrist*, makes clear, there are numerous people who, down through the years, received private revelations to do with the end times. However, many of them are overlooked here. All these limitations were due to the constraints of space, my

---

[14] Dispensationalism refers to a belief in a system of historical progression, as revealed in the Bible, consisting of a series of stages in God's self-revelation and plan of salvation. For an informed Protestant description of this aproach see, Dr Timothy Paul Jones's *Rose Guide to End Times Prophecy* (Peabody, MA: Rose Publishing, 2011).

[15] (Ben Lomond: Conciliar Press, 2005).

limited ability, and a desire not to overcomplicate what some readers may regard as an already complicated treatment of the subject. In spite of these provisos, it is my hope that this book will afford the reader a useful introduction to the, often neglected, subject of eschatology.

Stephen Walford ended his very helpful, *Heralds of the Second Coming*, by saying that the following words of Benedict XVI express why he wrote his book. I too can identify with them. 'Hope marks humanity's journey but for Christians it is enlivened by certainty: the Lord is present in the passage of our lives, he accompanies us and will one day also dry our tears. One day, not too far off, everything will find its fulfilment in the Kingdom of God, a Kingdom of justice and peace.'[16] Amen to that!

---

[16] (Tacoma WA: Angelico Press, 2013), 208.

ONE

CYCLICAL AND LINEAR TIME

THERE WAS A MEMORABLE SCENE in Stanley Kubrick's 1968 movie, 2001: A Space Odyssey. It depicted rival groups of ape-like creatures fighting at a water hole. Some of the apes, were holding bones in their hands and one of them seemed to have an eureka moment when he realised that he could use it as a weapon. Having beaten one of the enemy apes to death the others ran away. Then the weapon wielding ape threw the bone triumphantly into the air where it spun and finally morphed into a space craft. In this striking way Kubrick suggested that implicit in the first human insight was the latent capacity to reach for the stars. What was also implicit in the scene was the important notion of linear rather than a cyclical sense of time.

THE JEWS DISCOVER LINEAR TIME
In his book, *The Gifts of the Jews*, author Thomas Cahill points to the fact that ancient cultures such as the Incan, Mayan, Hopi – plus the Babylonians, Ancient Greeks, Hindus, Buddhists, Jainists, and others – had a concept of a wheel of time. They regarded it as cyclical and consisting of repeating ages that influenced every being in the Universe between birth and extinction. Belief in reincarnation as the endless transmigration of the soul into other body forms was an example of the cyclical view of time. As Henri-Charles Puech, a professor of the history of religion said of Greek thought, 'No event is unique, nothing is enacted, and will

be enacted perpetually; the same individuals have appeared, appear, and will appear at every turn of the circle.'[1]

In marked contrast the Jews developed a linear view of history. According to some of the doctors of the Church, salvation history consisted of six interrelated stages. The first was from Adam to the flood. The second, was from the flood to Abraham. The third was from Abraham to king David. The fourth was from king David to the Babylonian captivity. The fifth was from the Babylonian captivity to the coming of Jesus Christ. The sixth is from the first coming of Jesus to his second coming at the end of time. For Jews, Christians and Muslims time had a beginning in creation and will conclude in the end times. It was a narrative, whose triumphant conclusion would come in the future. From this insight came a new conception of men and women as individuals with unique destinies. In a very striking sentence Thomas Cahill says that the Jews were the first people to break out of the cyclical circle, to find a new way of thinking and experiencing, a new way of understanding and feeling about the world. Cahill writes, 'The moral is not that history repeats itself but that it is always something new: a process unfolding through time, whose direction and end we cannot know, except in so far as God gives us some hint of what is to come. The future will not be what has happened before; indeed, the only reality that the future has is that which has not happened yet.'[2] It can be said in passing that, of course, the Jews did recognise that there were cyclical patterns in life, for instance the recurring seasons and the waning and the waxing of the moon.

---

[1] 'Gnosis and Time,' in *Man and Time* (Princeton: Princeton University Press, 1957), 41.

[2] (New York: Anchor Books, 1998), 130-1.

But they saw these occurrences within the more general perspective of a linear view of history.

Science, which was born in the Christian West, was very much made possible and informed by the linear notion of history and the de-sacralisation of the natural world which had its own created autonomy. Fr Stanley Jaki, a renowned Benedictine priest with doctorates in theology and physics, was invited to give the Gifford Lectures in Edinburgh in 1975-6. In them he argued that a rational belief in the existence of a Creator, and of an ordered universe which God has created and governs, played a crucial role in the rise of science in Western culture and in all of its great creative advances. Surely that is particularly evident in modern cosmology and the theory of evolution.

COSMOLOGY: HAS THE UNIVERSE A PURPOSE?

Those who write about the origins of the universe have made astounding discoveries. They maintain that the universe originated about 13.7 billion years ago. Astrophysicists believe that before the big bang, the entire vastness of the observable universe, including all of its matter and radiation, was compressed into a hot, dense mass just a few millimeters across. It is referred to as a singularity. It is theorised to have existed for just a fraction of the first second of time.

Then a massive blast allowed all the universe's known matter and energy - even space and time themselves - to spring forth. Ever since then, the universe has been expanding with incomprehensible speed from its grapefruit-size origin to its mind boggling astronomical scope. The earth came into existence about four and a half billion years ago. Human life is thought to have emerged about 200,000 years ago. But excluding other kinds of disaster such as thermonuclear war, how long can life last on earth? We know that in about five billion years time the sun will become a red giant. At that point it will be so hot that life will no longer be possible here on earth. That reminds me of the story about a scientist who in the course of a lecture announced that the world as we know it would end in five billion years. One person in the audience put up his hand and asked, 'how long did you say life could last on earth?' 'Up to five billion years' replied the scientist, 'Thank God,' replied the audience member, 'for a moment there I thought you had said, four billion!'

For a time scientists had reason to think that the universe might eventually collapse back in on itself only to go through another big bang. However, according to a report published in Feb 2018 by the National Aeronautics and Space Administration in America, the latest scientific research indicates that the universe will go on expanding forever and will eventually become a cosmic graveyard because of the second law of thermodynamics. It states that the level of disorder in the universe is steadily increasing. Systems tend to move from ordered to more random behaviour as their energy is used up. These findings have discounted the possibility of a cyclical dynamic.

If these facts are understood in a purely naturalistic way they deprive life of any ultimate purpose or meaning. For example, well known atheist Stephen Weinberg, a Nobel Prize winner for physics, wrote, 'It is almost irresistible for humans to believe that we have some special relation to the universe, that human life is not just a more-or-less farcical outcome of a chain of accidents reaching back to the first three minutes, but that we were somehow built in from the beginning. ... It is very hard to realise that this is all just a tiny part of an overwhelmingly hostile universe. It is even harder to realise that this present universe has evolved from an unspeakably unfamiliar early condition, and faces a future extinction of endless cold or intolerable heat. The more the universe seems comprehensible, the more it also seems pointless.'[3]

While Stephen Weinberg, a materialist, sees no point in the universe, Walter Thirring, an Austrian physicist is the author of a book entitled, *Cosmic Impressions: Traces of God in the Laws of Nature*. In the preface he writes, 'In the end, reflection on the creation of the universe leads to reflections about the Creator, which may surprise some readers to hear. It is also common to hear the opinion that science leads to atheism. This is an opinion I can't share; I even find it somewhat absurd. When we are moved by a fantastic building, a cathedral or a mosque and have finally realised what is behind the glorious proportions, who would then say, 'Now we don't need the architect anymore. There might not even be one, this could all be the random product of circumstance?'[4] Later in the book Thirring says, 'Had the big bang been too weak and had everything collapsed, we would not exist. Had it been too powerful, everything would have dissipated too quickly, and again we would not exist.' He compares the origin of the world with a rocket that is supposed to put a satellite in orbit around the earth. He explains, 'If the rocket has too little push, it falls back to the earth, but if it has too much, it escapes into space.' He then adds that with the big bang the precision needed for bringing about our world was incomparably greater than that required for launching

[3] *The First Three Minutes* (New York: Bantam, 1979), 143-44.

[4] Quoted by Walter Thirring in *Cosmic Impressions: Traces of God in the Laws of Nature* (Philadelphia: Templeton Foundation Press, 2007), xii.

a satellite into orbit. The precision of this event is 'so far beyond man's power to conceive' that Professor Thirring exclaims, 'What an absurd idea that this should have happened by chance!'[5]

EVOLUTION: HAS LIFE A PURPOSE?

In his *Zoological Philosophy* (1809) Jean-Baptiste Lamarck proposed his teleological understanding of evolution, as ascent of the chain of being as a result of adaptation to the environment by means of inherited, acquired characteristics. However, when Charles Darwin published his *Origin of Species* in 1859, he stated that evolution had no purpose because it demonstrably occurred as a result of random mutations. While Darwin was clearly committed to the linear notion of history, he didn't believe that it had any teleology, i.e., plan or purpose. Echoing Darwin's belief, philosopher Daniel Dennett said, 'The only message in evolution is that the universe has no message.'[6] Jacques Monad, who won the Nobel Prize for medicine in 1965, wrote, in his book, *Chance and Necessity,* 'man at last knows that he is alone in the unfeeling immensity of the universe, out of which he emerged only by chance. Neither his destiny nor his duty have been written down. The kingdom above or the darkness below: it is for him to choose.'[7] In other words, although the train of evolution has left the station it isn't going anywhere in particular, there is neither an itinerary nor destination. One study of 149 leading biologists found that 89.9 percent believed that evolution has no ultimate purpose or goal except survival, and that we are just a cosmic accident existing at the whim of time and

---

[5] Ibid, 49.

[6] Quoted by John F. Haught, S.J., in *Christianity and Science: Toward a Theology of Nature* (Maryknoll, New York: Orbis Books, 2007), 60.

[7] (Glasgow: Collins Fontana Books, 1974), 167.

chance. A mere six percent believed that evolution has a purpose.[8] Almost all of those who believed that evolution had no purpose were atheists. The nihilistic implications of the Darwinian and neo-Darwinian viewpoints has found an echo in the writings of many influential contemporaries.

Jacques Monad was a friend of existentialist writer Albert Camus who won the Nobel Prize for literature in 1957. Both men were atheists. The latter got his ideas across in novels. I can remember reading *The Outsider* and *The Plague* when I was in my early twenties. While they were extremely well written, and had a certain nobility of thought and expression, they were ultimately nihilistic. For example, in 1936 Camus wrote to Claude de Fremenville, 'Basically, at the very bottom of life, which seduces us all, there is only absurdity, and more absurdity. And maybe that's what gives us our joy for living, because the only thing that can defeat absurdity is lucidity.'[9] Like his contemporary Jean Paul Sartre, Camus believed that we humans have no fixed essence. We become what we choose to do. In doing so, we create finite meanings in the midst of an absurd world. But those meanings are like the sand castles that children create on the beach. As soon as the waves of indifferent change wash over them they dissolve, so that in the end absurdity prevails. Camus's defiant but futile worldview reminds me of some lines of Welsh poet Dylan Thomas, 'Do not go gentle into that good night, old age should burn and rave at close of day; rage, rage against the dying of the light.' But not everyone has such a pessimistic world view.

---

[8]   Gregory W Graffin, *Evolution, Monism, Atheism, and the Naturalist World-View* (Ithaca, NY: Polypterus Press, 2004), 42.

[9] Quoted in John Strachan, *Poetry* (Edinburgh: University Press, 2011), 37.

In 2001 the Discovery Institute in the USA stated that during recent decades, new scientific evidence from many disciplines such as cosmology, physics, biology, 'artificial intelligence' research, and others had caused scientists to begin questioning a central tenet of Darwinian and neo-Darwinian natural selection. Yet public TV programmes, educational policy statements, and science textbooks have asserted that Darwin's theory of evolution fully explains the complexity of living things. The public has been assured that all known evidence supports Darwinism and that virtually every scientist in the world believes the theory to be true. Nevertheless, since 2001 more than 700 scientists have agreed with the following statement, 'We are sceptical of claims for the ability of random mutation and natural selection to account for the complexity of life. Careful examination of the evidence for Darwinian theory should be encouraged.'[10]

In his book *The Game*, Manfred Eigen, who won a Nobel Prize for science in 1967, said that 'the laws of nature direct chance'[11] In his book, *Evolution's Purpose: An Integral Interpretation of the Scientific Story of Our Origins*, author Steve McIntosh, a co-founder of a think tank, The Institute for Cultural Evolution, stated that the evolution of human consciousness and culture is the real focal point of evolution. Although it cannot be conflated with biological evolution, it is nevertheless the latest phase in the unfolding epic of evolution that can be traced all the way back to the original emergence of time and space in the big bang. When we view evolution from this macro perspective, we can begin to recognise

---

[10] Quoted by Simon Downing in *World Empire and the Return of Jesus Christ* (Maitland, FL: Xulon Press, 2011), 196.

[11] *Laws of the Game: How the Principles of Nature Govern Chance* (San Francisco: Harper & Row 1981),

it as an incontrovertibly purposeful phenomenon.[12] Francis Collins, an eminent American geneticist, moved from being an atheist to become a Christian believer. In June 2000 he was joined by President Bill Clinton in making the announcement of a working draft of the human genome, one of the greatest scientific break-throughs of all time. He stated that 'It is humbling for me, and awe-inspiring to realise that we have caught the first glimpse of our own instruction book, previously known only to God.'[13] In 2007 he published a book entitled, *The Language of God: A Scientist Presents Evidence for Belief*. Subsequently, in an interview he said that the overall aim of his book was to show that 'one can be intellectually in a rigorous position and argue that science and faith can be compatible,'[14] and that he had been prompted to write the book because 'most people are seeking a possible harmony between these worldviews [science and faith], and it seems rather sad that we hear so little about this possibility.'

Controversial Jesuit priest and scientist Teilhard de Chardin (1881-1955) would have agreed with McIntosh's and Collins' views.[15] He

---

[12] (New York: Select Books, 2012).

[13] Remarks made by President Clinton on the Completion of the First Survey of the Entire Human Genome Project June 26, 2000.

[14] Interview with D. J. Grothe on the Point of Inquiry podcast

[15] In 1962 the Holy Office issued a warning concerning the writings of Fr. Teilhard de Chardin, which was reiterated in 1981. It said, 'Several works of Fr. Pierre Teilhard de Chardin, some of which were posthumously published, are being edited and are gaining a good deal of success. The above-mentioned works abound in such ambiguities and indeed even serious errors as to offend Catholic doctrine... For this reason, the most eminent and most revered Fathers of the Holy Office exhort all Ordinaries as well as the superiors of Religious institutes, rectors of seminaries and presidents of universities, effectively to protect the minds, particularly of the youth,

avoided Darwinian reductionism. Instead he used to talk about evolutionary groping as *directed chance*. He believed that natural selection directs chance occurrences into adaptive channels. Typically, reductionists try to explain complex subjects, such as human consciousness, in terms of simpler constituent mechanisms and elements such as survival of the fittest and the electro-chemical activity of the brain. De Chardin realised that such a methodology had to be reversed. Simpler constituent elements, had to be understood in terms of the highest instances of evolution, such as human consciousness, and its pre-eminent activity of loving relationship with the world of people and things, and through both with God. He did not believe in a *deus ex machina*,[16] one who periodically intervenes in creation in a decisive way to bring about changes. As a scientist he believed that, from the moment of the big bang, billions of years ago, everything that we see today, was already present in a potential way. As a result he postulated that, because animals and humans are conscious, consciousness of a nascent kind must have been present in evolution from the beginning.[17] That led him to suggest that everything that exists has an inward, i.e., psychic element, co-extensive with it's without, i.e., its material complexity. He stated the law of complexity consciousness as

against the dangers presented by the works of Fr. Teilhard de Chardin and of his followers.' Despite the Church's continuing reservations about some aspects of his thought, in 1981, Cardinal Csaroli, Vatican Secretary of State, said that de Chardin's synthesis which is, 'often lyrical and animated with passion for the universal, will help to restore hope to those assailed by doubts.'

[16] The notion whereby a person or thing, for example in a detective movie, appears or is introduced suddenly and unexpectedly thereby providing a contrived solution to an apparently insoluble difficulty.

[17] It is not clear to me whether Teilhard believed in the traditional Catholic notion of the direct creation of each human soul by God.

follows: 'The degree of concentration of consciousness varies in inverse ratio to the simplicity of the material compound to which it corresponds. Or again: a consciousness is that much more perfected as it corresponds to a richer and better organised material edifice. Spiritual perfection and material synthesis are but two aspects or connected parts of one and the same phenomenon.'[18]

He also postulated that there were two kinds of energy involved in evolution, radial and tangential. Echoing Henri Bergson (1859-1941) he suggested that there is an obvious *elan* discernible in complexity consciousness. It is 'a combination of the play of chance [which is physical] and that of finality [which is psychic]'[19] In saying this he was breaking away from the Darwinian notion of blind, random mutations which have no teleological significance, in favour of an approach which was reminiscent, though different, from that of Lamarck. It is sometimes referred to as orthogenesis, i.e., in spite of the fact that evolution may operate through a mechanism of random mutations, viewed from a wider perspective it has a teleological purpose.

De Chardin was well aware that there are a number of texts in the writings of St Paul that can dovetail with the evolutionary under-standing of creation. In Rm 8:19-23 the apostle said, 'the creation waits with eager longing for the revealing of the sons of God. For the creation was subjected to futility, not willingly, but because of him who subjected it, in hope that the creation itself will be set free from its bondage to corruption and obtain the freedom of the glory of the children of God. For we know that the whole creation has been groaning together in the pains of childbirth until now. And

---

[18] *The Phenomenon of Man* (New York: Harper & Row, 1959), 62.

[19] *Activation of Energy* (New York: Harcourt Brace Jovanovich, 1963), 124.

not only the creation, but we ourselves, who have the first fruits of the Spirit, groan inwardly as we wait eagerly for adoption as sons, the redemption of our bodies.' In 1936, Teilhard de Chardin wrote a succinct summary of his thought,

> Christ possesses, by virtue of the mechanisms of the Incarnation, attributes which are universal and cosmic, and it is these which constitute him that personal Centre hypothetically invoked by the physics and metaphysics of evolution. *Such a perspective is in striking harmony with the most fundamental texts of St John and St Paul, and with the theology of the Greek Fathers* (my italics).[20]

In the prologue to his Gospel, John wished to show how the eternally, pre-existing Logos (Word) became incarnate. Jn 1:1 echoes Gen 1:1 and indicates that the incarnation of the Word initiates a new creation by making human salvation possible in a way that effects the whole of creation. In Rev 21:6, Christ is called 'the Alpha and the Omega, the beginning and the end.' Subsequently, de Chardin went on to refer to Christ as the Omega point in evolution. In 1924 he said that all the Pauline texts came down to two essential affirmations:

> 'In him all things hold together' (Col 1:17b) and 'You have been given fullness in Christ' (Col 2:10a), so that 'Christ is all and in all' (Col 3:11b). There we have the very definition of Omega.'[21]

---

[20] Christopher Mooney, *Teilhard de Chardin and the Mystery of Christ* (Garden City, New York: Image Books, 1968), 39-40.

[21] *Le Coeur de la Matiere*, (1950). An unpublished essay quoted by Christopher Mooney, *Teilhard de Chardin and the Mystery of Christ*, op. cit., 157.

De Chardin was influenced not only by Eph 4:9 but also by the following verse which reads: 'He who descended is he who ascended higher than all the heavens, *in order to fill the whole universe* [my italics].' From this Pauline idea he borrowed the notion of the *pleroma*, i.e., a Greek word which refers to the spiritual universe seen in terms of the full totality of the trans-figuring power of God in Christ. He wrote in a prayerful way:

> 'In a universe seen to be in a state of convergence, you have taken, by the presence of your Resurrection, the leading position of universal Centre in whom everything is gathered together.'[22]

Whether one agrees with de Chardin, or not, it is clear that the contemporary world view is evolutionary in nature. That was acknowledged in par. 5 of *Gaudium et Spes* (The Church in the Modern World), a key document of Vatican II. It said, 'the human race has passed from a rather static concept of reality to a more dynamic, evolutionary one.' In a 1996 message to the Pontifical Academy of Sciences, on evolution, Pope John Paul II said while quoting Pius XII in *Humani Generis* (Concerning some false opinions threatening to undermine the foundations of Catholic Doctrine) 'there is no conflict between evolution and the doctrine of the faith regarding man and his vocation, provided that we do not lose sight of certain fixed points.' Surprisingly, he added some time later, 'some new findings lead us toward the recognition of evolution *as more than an hypothesis.'*[23]

As a non scientist, it is not my aim to argue the relative merits and

---

[22] *Lexique Teilhard de Chardin* (Paris: Ed. Du Seuil, 1963), 71-2.

[23] *L'Osservatore Romano* 'Weekly Edition in English', Oct. 3rd (1996)

shortcomings of different scientific points of view.[24] What is clear however, is the fact that they all presume that time is linear. Furthermore, it seems to me that it is not unreasonable to argue from a scientific and a theological point of view that human history, like the evolving universe, has a providential and purposeful beginning, middle and end. As the author of Eph 1: 7-10 stated, 'In him we have redemption through his blood, the forgiveness of our trespasses, according to the riches of his grace, which he lavished upon us, in all wisdom and insight making known to us the mystery of his will, according to his purpose, which he set forth in Christ as a plan for the fullness of time, *to unite all things in him, things in heaven and things on earth.'*

HISTORY AND PROVIDENCE

When I studied politics and history for my B.A. in the 1960s I read a number of books by Cambridge historian Herbert Butterfield. A favourite of mine was his *Christianity and History* (1949) in which he described the unity of religion and history. He argued that the biblical concept of divine providence was a central one as far as history was concerned.[25] In a lecture he delivered in 1952 to students in Bangor University in Wales he identified three ways of

---

[24] For a brief critique of De Chardin's theory, cf. Pat Collins CM, 'Evangelisation as Inculturation in the Christology of Teilhard de Chardin,' *Milltown Studies*, no. 64 (Winter 2009): 76-99.

[25] It is worth mentioning that Butterfield wrote an influential book entitled, *The Origins of Modern Science 1300-1800* (New York: The Free Press, 1965). It concluded with this oft quoted sentence, 'There are times when we can never meet the future with sufficient elasticity of mind, especially if we are locked in the contemporary systems of thought. We can do worse than remember a principle which both gives us a firm rock and leaves us the maximum elasticity for our minds, the principle, Hold to Christ and for the rest be totally uncommitted.'

looking at history. The first is the 'biographical' way, in which we see that human beings freely choose and take responsibility for their actions. The second is the 'scientific' way, in which we see history as a realm of law necessitating what happens in a pre-determined manner. The third is the 'theological' way, in which we see God providentially at work in history in and through both personalities and processes. In this book I will be mainly pre-occupied by the third approach which focuses on salvation history.

Like Butterfield and de Chardin, I am convinced that the person of Jesus lies at the crosshairs of this conception of history. Firstly, the whole of the Old Testament anticipated his coming. Secondly, the messianic promises were fulfilled when Christ finally was born of the virgin Mary. Thirdly, from its earliest days the Christian Church has looked forward to the second coming of Christ when history will end and God's definitive victory will be consummated. Although the first two phases of salvation history are very important, they have already been completed. This book, therefore, is going to focus on the third by looking at what the prophecies in the Old and the New Testaments can tell us about the advent or the *parousia*[26] of Christ at an indeterminate point in the future. They will be augmented with the views of men and women who were party to private revelation which has the approval of the church.

CONCLUSION
Par. 302 of the *Catechism of the Catholic Church* states that God

---

[26] The word *'parousia'* is mainly used in Christian theology to refer to the second coming of Christ. It is derived from a Greek word meaning 'a coming' or 'a presence.'

created the universe 'in a state of journeying toward an ultimate perfection yet to be attained.' We refer to this purposeful path on which God has placed creation as Divine Providence. In short, Divine Providence can be defined as 'the dispositions by which God guides his creation toward this perfection.' That notion of providence as teleology[27] is implicit in an oft quoted verse in Jer 19:11, 'For I know the plans I have for you, declares the Lord, plans for welfare and not for evil, to give you a future and a hope.'

---

[27] The word *teleology*, is derived from the Greek word *telos*, meaning 'purpose' or 'end.' So teleology is the study of goals, ends, purposes, and destinies.

TWO

OLD TESTAMENT APOCALYPTIC

WHEN ONE READS THE OLD TESTAMENT it becomes apparent that the destruction of Jerusalem and the temple by Nebuchadnezzar in 587 BC had a profound effect on Jewish theology. The promises that had been given to David and his descendants had to be questioned in the light of events. What did God mean by saying that the throne and dynasty of David would last forever, when obviously it had just been toppled? Furthermore Jerusalem and the temple which played such a central role in the Torah, had been destroyed, and so sacrificial offerings had ceased. Therefore, the Babylonian exile was a really important watershed in the development of Jewish thinking. Was the Babylonian god more powerful than Yahweh? Or was there some other reason why the Jewish people had been led into exile? Maybe it wasn't God's fault. Maybe it was the people's responsibility, a punishment for their sins or the sins of their rulers. As a result of this kind of reflection about the trauma evoked by the destruction of Jerusalem and the Temple Jewish theology eventually gave birth to apocalyptic at about the time when traditional prophetic writing went into decline. It was a new form of prophetic literature which would illumine the contemporary crisis by looking forward to a future utopia when God would win a definitive victory over the forces of evil.

JEWISH APOCALYPTIC WRITINGS

It seems to me, that the Jewish notion of hope beyond hope was anticipated on many occasions, e.g., on the battlefield when the Israelites were confronted by much larger, better equipped armies. Nevertheless, they trusted that God was on their side. As a result, they would go into battle shouting the war cry of victory. As the Lord said prophetically in 2 Chron 20:15, 'Do not be afraid or discouraged because of this vast army. For the battle is not yours, but God's.'[1] As we read time and time again in the Old Testament, the Jews won numerous battles against all the odds. As a result they developed a theology which relied on interventions by God in order to overcome the overwhelming powers of evil arrayed against them. That notion was encapsulated in a verse which says, 'Be still, and know that I am God; I will be exalted among the nations, I will be exalted in the earth' (Ps 46:10).

It seems to me, that this kind of awareness informed Jewish apocalyptic writings, and strengthened and deepened their conviction that God would intervene in a transcendent and decisive way to finally vindicate the faithful in a manner which would defy all the odds stacked against them. One could refer to this perspective as apocalyptic eschatology. Writing about this topic David Aune stated, 'Apocalyptic eschatology is the narrative theology characteristic of apocalypses, centering in the belief that,

A. The present world order, regarded as both evil and oppressive, is under the temporary control of Satan and his human accomplices.
B. That this present evil world order will shortly be destroyed

---

[1] For more on this theme see Pat Collins, C.M., 'Delivering Cities, Towns and Localities from Territorial Spirits' in *Freedom from Evil Spirits* (Dublin: Columba, 2019), 201-232.

by God and replaced by a new and perfect order corresponding to Eden before the fall. During the present evil age, the people of God are an oppressed minority who fervently expect God, or his specially chosen agent the Messiah, to rescue them.'[2]

There are two main kinds of Old Testament apocalyptic. Firstly, we find it in an archetypal way in the Book of Daniel, especially chapters seven to twelve. Secondly, there are other books which contain proto-apocalyptic chapters such as Is 24–27; 33; 34–35; Jer 33:14–26; Ez 38–39; Joel 3:9–17; Zeph 1:15-18. For instance, in the latter we read,

'The great day of the Lord is near — near and coming quickly. Listen! The cry on the day of the Lord will be bitter the shouting of the warrior there. That day will be a day of wrath, a day of distress and anguish, a day of trouble and ruin, a day of darkness and gloom, a day of clouds and blackness, a day of trumpet and battle cry against the fortified cities and against the corner towers. I will bring distress on the people and they will walk like blind men, because they have sinned against the Lord. Their blood will be poured out like dust and their entrails like filth. Neither their silver nor their gold will be able to save them on the day of the Lord's wrath. In the fire of his jealousy the whole world will be consumed, for he will make a sudden end of all who live in the earth.'

---

[2] David Aune, 'Understanding Jewish and Christian Apocalyptic' Word & World Volume 25, Number 3,(Summer 2005): 236. In the fourth of his 2018 Gifford Lectures, entitled, 'The End of the World? Eschatology and Apocalyptic,' Bishop Tom Wright described seven contemporary under-standings of eschatology and six of apocalyptic. See https://www.youtube .com/watch?reload=9&v=DHubt-njRlM (retrieved 31/1/2019).

Jewish scripture scholar Christine Hayes, who lectures in the religious studies department of Yale University, maintains that the Book of Daniel is the only truly apocalyptic book in the Old Testament. She suggests, in an illuminating way, that apocalyptic literature has the following characteristics:[3]

1. *Pseudonmy*, i.e., most apocalyptic writings are attributed to important figures from the past.
2. *Mediated revelation*, i.e., knowledge is mediated through a heavenly messenger or angel by means of visions or dreams.
3. *Symbolism*, i.e., apocalyptic writings are symbolic and employ strange and bizarre images of beasts and monsters.
4. *Catastrophe*, i.e., apocalypses predict catastrophes to come, which represent the coming of the end.
5. *Dualism*, i.e., apocalypses divide humankind into two opposing groups: the righteous who are a tiny minority, and the wicked, who are the vast majority (cf. Mt 7:14).
6. *Divine king*, i.e., God usually appears in an apocalypse as an enthroned king who brings all history to a dramatic end.
7. *Mythological elements*, i.e., apocalyptic writings often employ mythological themes and motifs, especially that of a battle between God and chaotic, evil forces in its depiction of the final battle.
8. *Judgment and life after death.*, i.e., apocalypses generally depict a judgment of the individual dead, followed by everlasting life or punishment.
9. *Despair and hope*, i.e., it affirms that God will intervene in human history and set at rights all that is wrong by interrupting the natural order and destroying the world as we know it in order to rescue the righteous and humble the wicked.

---

[3] Christine Hayes, 'Postexilic Prophecy and the Rise of Apocalyptic' in *Introduction to the Bible* (New Haven: Yale University Press, 2012), 382-383.

Prophecy and apocalyptic

While prophecy and apocalyptic are related, because both of them are the result of divine revelation, they are in fact distinct. According to scripture scholar David Aune, prophecy can be defined as, 'intelligible messages from God in human language through inspired human mediums, prophecy can assume a wide variety of forms.'[4] In words that echo those of Christine Hayes, David Aune says that apocalyptic is, 'A form of revelatory literature in which the author narrates both the visions he has purportedly experienced and their meaning, usually elicited through a dialogue between the seer and an interpreting angel. The substance of these revelatory visions is the immanent intervention of God in human affairs to bring the present evil world system to an end and to replace it with an ideal one. This transformation is accompanied by the punishment of the wicked and the reward of the righteous.'[5]

Aune goes on to describe the difference between prophecy and apocalyptic. He says that God does not reveal his word directly to the apocalyptists, as Yahweh did to the Old Testament prophets, but indirectly through visions and scripture, both of which require interpretation. Daniel was an example of someone who received this form of revelation. The prophets tried to translate their revelations so that they would impact on the religious, political and social realities of the time. The prophetic word was addressed directly to the people which left open the possibility of repentance and a change of heart which might cause God to act in a way that was different from the one that had been declared. But apocalyptic

---

[4] David Aune, *Prophecy in Early Christianity and the Ancient Mediterranean World* (Grand Rapids: Erdmans, 1983), 103.

[5] Ibid, 108.

predictions reflected an unconditional verdict which is fixed in the pre-determined purposes of God.[6]

DANIEL'S APOCALYPTIC

As far as modern Jewish and Gentile readers are concerned, the Book of Daniel is the most important apocalyptic book in the Old Testament. Among other things it contains a remarkable prophecy (Dan 9:24-27) which appears to predict in a coded way that the Messiah would appear about 26 AD, precisely the date that many scholars give for Jesus' baptism by John. For a good exposition of this interpretation see Roy Shoeman's succinct explanation in *Salvation is from the Jews: The Role of Judaism in Salvation History from Abraham to the Second Coming.*[7]

Daniel, who was exiled to Babylon, was a contemporary of Ezekiel. Although Jesus Christ spoke about Daniel's *function* as prophetic (Matt. 24:15), his position was that of governmental official and inspired writer, rather than as a ministering prophet. The second part of his book was apocalyptic in nature. There has been quite a debate about when it was written. It is an important point because it determines how the apocalyptic symbolism should be interpreted. So we begin by looking at what reputable scholars have to say about the date of its composition.

In the introduction to the Book of Daniel in the *New International Version, Zondervan Study Bible,* we read, 'The book was probably

---

[6] See, Niels Christian Hvidt, 'The Relationship Between Prophetic and Apocalyptic Literature' in *Christian Prophecy: The Post-biblical Tradition* (New York: Oxford University Press, 2007), 47.

7 (San Francisco: Ignatius Press, 2004), 81-83.

completed c. 530 BC,[8] shortly after Cyrus the Great, King of Persia, captured the city of Babylon in 539.' It goes on to add, 'The notes in this study Bible assume that Daniel received these visions from God in the sixth century B.C.' *The New Oxford Annotated Bible* says that Daniel's prophetic statements of an apocalyptic kind were most likely composed either in the late Persian era (350-333 BC) or the early Hellenistic era (333-170 BC). That is a wide span of dates ranging between 350 and 170 BC.[9] The *English Standard Version Study Bible* says that, 'Some scholars have argued that the book must be a second century document. . . However the facts do not require a late date. In the first place, current knowledge of the sixth-century B.C. history is far from complete, and there are plausible harmonisations that explain the alleged discrepancies.'[10] It can be said that this would accord with the traditional Catholic position. For example, in his book *Antichrist*, St. Robert Bellarmine, S.J., like many of the doctors and Fathers of the Early Church, opted for the early date.

The majority of contemporary scholars tend to opt for a later second century date. In a *Wikipedia* article on the Book of Daniel we read, 'The prophecies of Daniel are accurate down to the career of Antiochus IV Epiphanes, king of Syria and oppressor of the Jews, but not in its prediction of his death: the author seems to know about Antiochus' two campaigns in Egypt (169 and 167 BC), the desecration of the Temple (the 'abomination of desolation'), and the

[8] *New International Version Zondervan Study Bible* (Grand Rapids: Zondervan, 2015), 1687.

[9] *The Oxford Annotated Bible, New Revised Edition with the Apocrypha* (New York: Oxford University Press, 2010), 1233.

[10] *English Standard Version Study Bible* (Wheaton Illinois: Crossway, 2011), 1581.

fortification of the Akra (a fortress built inside Jerusalem), but he seems to know nothing about the reconstruction of the Temple or about the actual circumstances of Antiochus' death in late 164 BC. Chapters 10–12 of Daniel must therefore have been written between 167 and 164 BC. There are other scholars who opt for the later date of composition for historical reasons, e.g., the Wisdom of Sirach, a work dating from around 180 BC, draws on almost every book of the Old Testament except Daniel.

Some contemporary scholars seem to opt for the late second century date of composition partly because of linguistic reasons and also because of a modern philosophical assumption that long range predictive prophecy is impossible. Therefore all the predictions in Daniel, must necessarily have been composed in the 2nd century BC, when their fulfilment had already taken place. So for them the Book of Daniel is merely offering an inspired interpretation of those events. This view is referred to in Latin as *vaticinium ex eventu*, i.e., foretelling an event after it has already occurred. Although there are valid arguments for the earlier and later dating of the Book of Daniel, I am inclined to opt for the former.

A] DAN 7:1-8

At this point we are going to focus on chapter seven. Unlike the preceding ones, it was written in Aramaic. Daniel reported an apocalyptic vision he himself had experienced. He saw four animals, a lion, bear, leopard and fierce beast who represented four kingdoms which paralleled, the four kingdoms symbolised in King Nebuchadnezzar's dream which was described in Dan 2: 31-45. At this point scripture scholars differ in their interpretation of Daniel's vision.

As was noted above, most contemporary exegetes, who employ the historical critical method, believe that the Book of Daniel was written sometime between 167 and 164 BC. As we saw, there are other exegetes who opt for a much earlier date of composition. Whereas those who opt for the later date say that the animals mentioned by Daniel represent the Babylonian, the Mede, Persian, and Greek, kingdoms, those who opt for the earlier date maintain that the animals represent the Babylonian, the Medo-Persian, Greek, and Roman kingdoms. By and large, the Fathers of the Church, e.g., Cyril of Alexandria, John Chrysostom, Augustine and later Robert Bellarmine accepted this second interpretation. One's understanding of Daniel's prophecy, however, depends on which of these two interpretations is chosen.

If one adopts the later date of composition, then the fourth beast represents the Greeks and particularly the Seleucids of Syria. The little horn, therefore, is identified as the Greek king Antiochus Epiphanes IV. The three horns plucked up by this little horn are easily understood to be the Greek kings who were killed by Antiochus Epiphanes. The time of 'three and a half years' mentioned in Dan 7:25 exactly coincides with the period of the Jewish Maccabean Revolt against the Greek armies of Antiochus from 167-164 BC. The First and Second books of Maccabees independently refer to the one who made 'alterations in times and in laws' (Dan 7:25) as the Greek tyrant Antiochus did (cf. 1 Macc 1:45; 2 Macc 6:6). If this modern interpretation is adopted, the prophecy has very little on-going apocalyptic relevance because it has already been fulfilled. That said, the evil perpetrated by Antiochus, could be seen as a symbolic intimation of an anti-Christ figure to come in the end times.

But if one opts for the earlier date of composition, which is supported by some respected scholars, where the fourth animal represents the Roman Empire, then Daniel's apocalyptic prophecy has yet to be fully fulfilled. Sad to say, ever since the Reformation many Protestant writers have suggested that the small horn, which represents the Antichrist, is a symbol of the Pope, the head of the Roman Catholic church. Martin Luther declared ... 'We are of the conviction that the Papacy is the seat of the real antichrist.'[11] Speaking about the Roman pontiff, John Calvin declared ... 'I deny him to be the vicar of Christ .... He is antichrist - I deny him to be head of the church.'[12] John Knox stated, 'That tyranny which the pope himself has for so many ages exercised over the church, the very antichrist and son of perdition of whom Paul speaks.'[13] John Wesley opined, 'Roman Papacy, the antichrist is, in an emphatic sense, the man of sin.'[14] *The Westminster Confession* of the Church of England states, 'There is no other head of the church but the Lord Jesus Christ; nor can the pope of Rome in any sense be the head thereof; but is that Antichrist, that man of sin, and that son of perdition, that exalts himself in the church against Christ, and all that is called God.' Those who have been influenced by this offensive and unwarranted Protestant interpretation need to know that it was convincingly critiqued by St Robert Bellarmine (1542-

---

[11] Quoted by Le Roy Froom, in *The Prophetic Faith of Our Fathers*, Vol.2, (Washington: Review & Herald, 1978),256.

[12] John Calvin *Tracts*, Vol. 1, (Calvin Translation Society , 1844), 219,220.

[13] *The Zurich Letters*, p.199

[14] Quoted by Albert Close in, *Antichrist and His Ten Kingdoms* (London: Thynne and Co, 1917), 110.

1621), and Cardinal Edward Henry Manning (1808-1892).[15] To them the little horn represents the Antichrist who is yet to come perhaps from one of the countries that emerged from the former Roman Empire.

B] DAN 12:2-3

Dan 12:2-3 is another eschatological passage. It says,

> 'And many of those who sleep in the dust of the earth shall awake, some to everlasting life, and some to shame and everlasting contempt. And those who are wise shall shine like the brightness of the sky above; and those who turn many to righteousness, like the stars forever and ever.'

For most of their history in Old Testament times, the Jews didn't really believe in an afterlife. Here Daniel talks about the resurrection of the righteous and the non-righteous to life eternal (i.e., after Christ's second coming). When the righteous are raised from the dead, they will shine like the brightness of the heavens' and be 'like the stars for ever and ever.'

Jesus referred to the prophecy of Daniel when he said in Mt 24:15, 'When you see the desolating abomination spoken through Daniel the prophet standing in the holy place then those in Judea must flee to the mountains.' This is a clear reference to the destruction of Jerusalem as a symbol of the Second Coming. In a footnote the *New*

---

[15] Like Cardinal Newman, Cardinal Manning a convert from the Anglican Church rejected the notion that the Pope was the Antichrist. His ideas were expressed in *'The Present Crisis in the Holy See'* (London: Burns & Lampert, 1861). The book's four chapters, 'The Progress of the Mystery of Iniquity,'... ...'The Antichrist,' 'What Holds Back the Antichrist' and 'The Apostasy of Rome' warned of an impending crisis facing the Church.

International Version Cultural Background Study Bible says, 'Historically, when God's people persisted in disobedience, God allowed the temple to be desecrated (an abomination) and ultimately destroyed (desolation). The pattern is most obvious in Daniel (cf Da 8:13; 9:27; 11:31).' Whereas some verses may refer to the anti Jewish actions of Antiochus Epiphanes IV or later to the destruction of the temple in 70 AD by the Romans under the leadership of Titus, Dan 12:11 sounds as if it ultimately refers to the end times which those historical events prefigured. For example, the destruction of the temple in 70 AD, can be interpreted as an anticipatory metaphor for the final tribulation.

EZEKIEL'S APOCALYPTIC

It is thought that the prophet Ezekiel, a priest, was born in Babylon around 622 BC. He was one of the many Jews who ended up in exile following the destruction of Jerusalem in 597 BC. He received his call to be a prophet in that city. In chapters 38 and 39 of his book, which I'd encourage you to read, Ezekiel made three interrelated prophecies (38:2-13; 14-23; 39:1-20). These were not only relevant for the people of his time, they also had an apocalyptic dimension. I can well believe those scripture scholars who maintain that they are among the most difficult chapters in the Bible to interpret.

It could be argued that these prophecies were partially fulfilled during the Old Testament period when the Jews exiled in Babylon returned to Israel in 538 BC, and again when the Maccabees defeated the powerful armies of King Antiochus Epiphanes in 164 BC. Nevertheless, it has been suggested that Ezekiel's prophecy was never completely fulfilled by historical events. As a result, the Old Testament events already mentioned were also symbolic anticipations of apocalyptic events that would take place at the end of history.

Instead of going into all the intricacies of the biblical interpretation, which quite frankly can be confusing, Ezekiel predicted a time when there would be an attack on the promised land by the embodiment of evil from the North. Following a cataclysmic, doomsday battle, God would be acknowledged by all the nations as the undisputed victor. At this point in his book, Ezekiel's prophecies of restoration, which aimed to reverse preceding tragedies, have not yet reversed Israel's Babylonian destruction. The Northern enemy mentioned here is probably an end-time replacement for Babylon, and about any superpower that would presume to challenge the sovereignty of God. Gog will be defeated both in the battle field and back at home. God's holy name will be vindicated. The huge quantities of war material which were mentioned indicate that this is an apocalyptic rather than an historical victory.

It seems to me that there is a link between chapters 38 and 39 and the line in the Lord's Prayer which says, 'Our Father in heaven *may your name be kept holy*' (Mt 6:9). Believers are inclined to think that, first and foremost, this phrase means that they should praise and honour God's holy name. However, its deeper and more fundamental meaning is rooted in Ezekiel's prophetic conviction that God would show forth the holiness of the divine name by intervening in a definitive way when Israel was being attacked by the forces of Gog, i.e., by demonic evil. As the Lord says to them, 'O Gog, I will bring you against my land, so that the nations may know me when I show myself holy through you before their eyes . . . I will show my greatness and my holiness, and I will make myself known in the sight of many nations. Then they will know that I am the Lord' (Ezek 38:16; Ezek 38:23). This promise is reminiscent of an incident in Ex 14:14 which describes how the Jewish people were faced by the might of the Egyptian army. But Moses said to them, 'Do not be afraid. Stand firm and you will see the deliverance the Lord will bring you today . . . The Lord will fight for you; you need only be still.' As John Meier says in his commentary on Mt 6:9, 'For Jesus, the Father reveals his transcendent holiness precisely by bringing in his eschatological kingdom, by assuming his rightful rule over the world. . . The resplendent theophany Jesus thinks of is the appearing of God on the last day; the Our Father is an eschatological prayer, a prayer that God will hasten the end time.'

There seems to be a reference to Ezekiel's apocalyptic in the account of how the enemy will go out to deceive the nations in the four corners of the earth - Gog and Magog - to gather them for battle.[16] In number they are like the sand on the seashore.

'They marched across the breadth of the earth and surrounded the camp of God's people, the city he loves. But fire came down from heaven and devoured them. And the devil, who deceived them, was thrown into the lake of burning sulphur, where the beast and the false prophet had been thrown. They will be tormented day and night for ever and ever.' (Rev 20:9-10).

Commenting on these verses the *New International Version Cultural Backgrounds Study Bible* says, 'In many Jewish texts Gog serves as

---

[16] On the issue of Gog and Magog see Joseph L. Iannuzzi, *Antichrist and the End Times* (McKees Rock PA: St Andrew's Productions, 2005), 93-98.

a mythical function; in some texts, various evil oppressors could fill the role of the final 'Gog' if God intended their day as the end of time. Jewish writers typically used the invasion of Gog to predict the gathering of all nations against Israel, and Revelation likely employs this image in a similar way.'

It should be said that reputable scripture scholars are critical of some modern commentators such as Protestant writers Chuck Missler and Hans Lindsey who rather arbitrarily suggest that the forces of evil from the North can be identified with contemporary countries such as Turkey and Russia together with their Muslim allies. Some of them go so far as to interpret Ezek 38:22 as a reference to Word War III during which Israel will be attacked, possibly with nuclear weapons. However, there is no convincing evidence that Ezekiel had any of this in mind. Most scholars believe that Ezekiel was not referring to specific modern nations but in a symbolic way to demonic powers: 'spiritual forces of evil in the heavenly realms' (Eph 6:12).

THE RETURN OF ENOCH AND ELIJAH

According to the Old Testament, two people, Enoch and Elijah did not see death but were translated to paradise.[17] Enoch is described as a man who 'walked with God for 300 years' (Gen 5:23). In Gen 5:24 we are told that rather than having to die, 'then he was no

---

[17] Like St Hildegarde Bl. Catherine Emmerich suggested that 'Enoch and Elias are in paradise' but not in the heavenly realm proper to the saints and angels, but in the paradisal garden that Adam and Eve left unspoiled and awaiting the day when God will call upon them to oppose the Antichrist. See *The Life of Jesus Christ and Biblical Revelation*, Vol 1, (Rockford Ill: Tan Books, 2003), 556-564. St Thomas Aquinas made a similar point in *Summa Theologiae III*, q. 49, a. 5.

more, because God took him away.' In Sir 44:15 we are told that Enoch was transferred to Paradise, 'so that he might offer repentance to the nations.' Speaking about the great prophet Elijah 2 Kings 2:11 tells us that, 'Suddenly a chariot of fire and horses of fire appeared and . . . Elijah went up to heaven in a whirlwind.' The prophet Malachi spoke about a return of Elijah. 'Behold, I will send you Elijah the prophet before the coming of the great and dreadful day of the Lord.' (Mal 4:5, 6)

The Jews expected Elijah to be the precursor of the Messiah. Speaking about John the Baptist, Jesus said in Matt 17:12, 'I tell you, Elijah has already come, and they did not recognise him.' However, when John the Baptist himself was asked in John 1:21 'Then who are you? Are you Elijah?' He said, 'I am not.' Jesus was talking symbolically, and John was talking literally. Elijah is mentioned in a few other places in the Gospels. Firstly, in the Lk 9:28-36 we are told that Elijah and Moses appeared and conversed with Jesus as representatives of the law and the prophets respectively. Secondly, in Mk 8:27-28, we are told that, 'Jesus and his disciples went on to the villages around Caesarea Philippi. On the way he asked them, 'Who do people say I am?' They replied, 'Some say John the Baptist; others say Elijah; and still others, one of the prophets.' Thirdly, in Mt 27:46-47 we are told that when Jesus cried out, 'My God, my God, why have you forsaken me?' some of the bystanders said, 'He's calling Elijah.'

In Rev 11:3, speaking about the end times, we are told that the Lord said, 'I will give power to my two witnesses, and they will prophesy for 1,260 days, clothed in sackcloth.' Who are the two witnesses referred to? Many Fathers and doctors of the Church say that they are Enoch and Elijah who will return before the second coming of Jesus. Adso Abbot of Montier-en-Der (c.915-992) wrote a letter to Gerberga, sister of Otto I and wife of Louis IV of West Francia. It exerted great influence in Europe for centuries afterwards. In it he wrote,

'Lest the Antichrist come suddenly and without warning and deceive and destroy the whole human race by his error, before his arrival the two great prophets Enoch and Elijah will be sent into the world. They will defend God's faithful against the attack of the Antichrist with divine arms and will instruct, comfort, and prepare the elect for battle with three and a half years teaching and preaching. These two very great prophets and teachers will convert the sons of Israel who will live in that time to the faith, and they will make their belief unconquerable among the elect in the face of the affliction of so great a storm. At that time what scripture says will be fulfilled 'If the number of sons of Israel be like the sand of the sea, their remnant will be saved.' When, after three and a half years, they shall have finished their preaching, the Antichrist's persecution will soon begin to blaze out. He will first take up his arms against them and will slay them, as it says in the Apocalypse: 'And when they have finished their witness the beast which will ascend from the abyss will make war against them and will conquer and kill them.' After these two have been slain, he will then persecute the rest of the faithful, either by making them glorious martyrs or by rendering them apostates. And whoever shall have believed in him will receive his brand on the forehead.'[18]

---

[18] See Bernard McGinn, 'Adso's biography of Antichrist,' in *Antichrist: Two Thousand Years of the Human Fascination with Evil* (San Francisco: Harper Collins, 1994), 100-103.

When our Lady appeared at La Salette in the 19th century she said to Maximin: 'They [Enoch and Elijah] will suddenly appear on earth full of the spirit of God, when the Church becomes darkened and the world in terrible agony. They will convert those of good will and comfort the oppressed Christians. With the help of the Holy Spirit, they will have great success against the heresies of the Antichrist. But in the end they will be delivered unto death.' Speaking to Melanie, Mary said, 'The Church will be eclipsed, the world will be in consternation. But behold Enoch and Elijah filled with the Spirit of God will preach with the strength of God, and men of good, will believe in God, and many souls will be consoled; they will make great progress.'[19] It is thought that Enoch will evangelise and organise the Jews who will seek baptism and convert to the Christian faith during the reign of the Antichrist. Elijah will organise the last wave of Gentile evangelisation and conversion to Christ during the Antichrist's reign of terror. Both prophets will finally be slain, rise again, and ascend to Heaven as explained in Apoc 11:9-11.

SOME OTHER OLD TESTAMENT TEXTS

Arguably there are some other Old Testament texts which can be interpreted in an eschatological way. Here are two of many possible examples:

- In Zech 13:8-9 we read that at some point before the second coming of Christ two thirds of the Jewish people will be killed. That text may have been fulfilled during the

---

[19] Apparition of the Blessed Virgin on the Mountain of La Salette the 19th of September, 1846. Published by the Shepherdess of La Salette with the Imprimatur of the Bishop of Lecce, part III. http://thepopeinred.com/secret.htm (Accessed 5/2/2019)

Holocaust when between 60 and 72 per cent of Europe's Jews perished and many of them were cremated in fire.
• Roy Schoeman cites texts, Zech 12:1-3 and Joel 3:2 which may indicate that a fight over Jerusalem will cause a world war, perhaps as a prelude to the end times. Zech 12: 6-9 suggests that when the war breaks out, Israel will have miraculous strength and will be able to defend itself.

CONCLUSION

One of the aims of this book is to identify anticipatory signs of a prophetic kind that would indicate that the second coming of Jesus is imminent. It would seem from Ezekiel's writings that the battle he said would take place at the end of time would be a spiritual one. The nations he mentioned were symbols of the dark powers in every age – spiritual powers that will seek, right up to the very end of time, to destroy the people of God. If one believes that the Book of Daniel was written around 530 BC and that mention of the fourth kingdom refers to the Roman rather than the Greek empire, then there is the possibility that the antichrist will be a leader from one of the ten nations that emerged from the Roman Empire.

Isaac Newton was one of the greatest scientists and mathematicians of all time. What is not so well known is the fact that he was very interested in biblical prophecy and apocalyptic. In 1733 he published a book entitled, *Observations upon the Prophecies of Daniel and the Apocalypse of St John*. Having examined the Book of Daniel Newton came to the conclusion that 1260 years would elapse between the re-establishment of the Holy Roman Empire by Charlemagne in 800 A.D. and the end times. He calculated therefore that the end of the world would occur in 2060. He added that it may end later but not sooner. I suspect that modern scripture scholars would be very sceptical of such a claim. That said, many would agree with a statement he made about the end-times, 'if God was so angry with the Jews for not searching more diligently into the prophecies which he had given them to know Christ by, why should we think he will excuse us for not searching the prophecies which he has given us to know Antichrist by?'

THREE

JESUS AND THE END-TIMES

ERHAPS THE MOST ADEQUATE ANSWER to Jesus' question, 'Who do you say that I am?' is that he is the eschatological prophet who proclaimed and inaugurated God's definitive entry into human history, the reign of God which meant the imminent end of the old world order.[1] At the time of Jesus, apocalyptic thinking and writing were common in Jewish circles. Messianic expectation was at fever pitch because the Jewish people had learned from chapter nine of the Book of Daniel, to expect the messiah any day soon.[2] Not only that, they were undergoing a time of great hardship as a result of the occupation of the pagan Romans. It was a period of political and religious unrest, the kind that was conducive to apocalyptic thinking and writing. For example when the Dead Sea Scrolls of the Essene community (2nd century BC to the 1st century AD) were discovered in the caves of Qumran between 1947-56 AD, one of them was the *War Rule*. It contained an apocalyptic prophecy which described an impending war between the Sons of Light and the Sons of Darkness. It stated that in the end, as a result of divine intervention, the children of darkness would be destroyed so that the children of light could live in peace for all eternity.

---

[1] Cf. Ropes, Gray, Kaveny, & Keenan, 'Jesus and Christian Ethics' in *Theological Studies*, no. 56, (1995), 96.

[2] For more on this point see Roy H Schoeman, *Salvation is from the Jews* (San Francisco: Ignatius, 2003), 81-83.

It could be argued that John the Baptist was an eschatological prophet who was influenced by this kind of thinking. It is even said that he may have been a member of the Qumran community. During his public ministry he was the new Elijah spoken about in Mal 4:5–6 where we read, 'Behold, I will send you Elijah the prophet before the coming of the great and dreadful day of the Lord: And he shall turn the heart of the fathers to the children, and the heart of the children to their fathers, lest I come and smite the earth with a curse.' As Jesus testified in Mt 11:14, John was the new Elijah. It was he who would announce the coming of 'the great and dreadful day of the Lord,' That reference is apocalyptic in nature and refers to the end time when God would intervene in human history to overcome evil and firstly to judge, and then to punish, or reward human beings.

Jesus was a disciple of John. Although, like his cousin, he was an eschatological prophet, he preached a less austere, more merciful message. Well known scripture scholar, Reginald Fuller has argued that the category of the eschatological prophet remains the best category for understanding Jesus' historical mission which 'gives a unity to all of Jesus' historical activity, his proclamation, his teaching with authority, his healings and exorcisms, his conduct in eating with the outcast, and finally his death in the fulfilment of his prophetic mission. Take the implied self-understanding of his role in terms of the eschatological prophet away, and the whole ministry falls into a series of unrelated, if not meaningless fragments.'[3]

A number of years ago I read John Meier's excellent commentary on the Gospel of Matthew. I was really surprised by what he said

---

[3] Reginald Fuller, *Foundations of New Testament Christology* (New York: Charles Scribner's Sons 1965), 109.

about the Lord's prayer. He suggested that it can only be properly interpreted in the light of the second coming. He maintained that, 'the Our Father is an eschatological prayer, a prayer that God will hasten the end time.' For example, commenting on the words, 'thy will be done,' (Mt 6:10) he said, 'The death-resurrection for Matthew is the climax of the eschatological drama of Jesus; it is the turning of the ages. And so Jesus teaches his disciples to pray that God will bring this eschatological crisis to its consummation.' When we pray, 'Give us this day our daily bread,' Meier suggests that this particular petition, 'may reflect the yearning for God's definitive, once-and-for-all act on the last day. If this is so, the bread refers to the final banquet, in the kingdom, which is urgently requested even for today.' In the course of an interview John Meier said, 'What seems so central in Jesus' teaching... is that he is speaking of a future coming of the kingdom of God, a consummation of Israel's history in the apparently near future, that would bring about a radical change in human life. This change would not be brought about so much by human effort but by a definitive action of God at the end of time, at least time as we know it. 'Thy kingdom come' is a very central petition of the Lord's Prayer itself.'[4]

WAS JESUS MISTAKEN ABOUT THE END OF THE WORLD?

In his Mount of Olives discourse, Jesus said, 'From the fig tree learn its lesson: as soon as its branch becomes tender and puts out its leaves, you know that summer is near. So also, when you see all these things, you know that he is near, at the very gates. Truly, I say to you, this generation will not pass away until all these things

---

[4] Finding the Historical Jesus: An Interview with John P. Meier. https://www.franciscanmedia.org/finding-the-historical-jesus-an-interview-with-john-p-meier/ (Accessed 29/4/2019). See also Brant Pitre, 'Jesus, the Messianic Banquet, and the Kingdom of God,' in *Letter & Spirit* 5 (2009): 145–166.

take place' (Mt 24:32-34). Speaking about this verse, a number of notable scholars say that it proves that Jesus was a failed apocalyptic prophet who believed that the world would end within a generation. For example C. S. Lewis said that it was, 'the most embarrassing verse in the Bible.'[5] British philosopher Bertrand Russell, wrote a book entitled, *Why I am Not a Christian* in which he said that one of the reasons he was not a believer was because he could not have faith that Jesus was divine due to the fact that he was quite clearly wrong about the end of the world. Albert Schweitzer, author of the influential book *The Quest of the Historical Jesus* said that Jesus was a failed 'apocalyptic prophet.' In view of the fact that Deut 17:19-22 says that if the predictions of a seer are not fulfilled, he or she is a to be regarded as a false prophet, do the apocalyptic words of Jesus invalidate his claims about himself and his second coming?

Few chapters of the Bible have evoked more disagreement among interpreters than Matthew 24 and its parallels in Mark 13 and Luke 21. When we listen to and understand what Jesus said on the Mount of Olives we find that he spoke about two interrelated subjects, the destruction of Jerusalem and its majestic temple, and the end times. While they are separate topics, it seems pretty clear that Jesus saw the destruction of the temple as a sort of metaphor for the tribulation that would occur at the end of history as we know it. Catholic scripture scholar Brant Pitre has offered a very clear explanation of this discourse, in a four disc DVD series entitled, *Jesus and the End Times: the Catholic View of the Last Days*. He maintains, in a persuasive way, that the eminent scholars already referred to, got the mistaken impression that what Jesus

---

[5] C.S. Lewis, *The World's Last Night: And Other Essays* (New York: Harcourt, Brace & Co., 1952), .97

said about the end-times would occur within a generation. Actually he was talking about the immanent destruction of Jerusalem and its temple which would take place within a generation. It would inaugurate the new covenant which would come to an end with the second coming of Jesus at the end of time. My comments on Jesus' words are heavily indebted to Pitre's exegesis even though I am aware that other scripture scholars would disagree with his interpretation.

JESUS PREDICTED THE DESTRUCTION OF JERUSALEM AND THE TEMPLE
Three apocalyptic discourses are attributed to Jesus and as a result are of central importance. They are to be found in Mt 24:1-35; Mk 13:1-32; Lk 17:22-37. We will focus on the Olivet discourse of Jesus in Matthew's gospel Here is the passage with its associated verse numbers so that they can be referred to below.

'Jesus left the temple and was going away, when his disciples came to point out to him the buildings of the temple. 2) But he answered them, 'You see all these, do you not? Truly, I say to you, there will not be left here one stone upon another that will not be thrown down.' 3) As he sat on the Mount of Olives, the disciples came to him privately, saying, 'Tell us, when will these things be, and what will be the sign of your coming and of the close of the age?' 4) And Jesus answered them, 'See that no one leads you astray. 5) For many will come in my name, saying, 'I am the Christ,' and they will lead many astray. 6) And you will hear of wars and rumours of wars. See that you are not alarmed, for this must take place, but the end is not yet. 7) For nation will rise against nation, and kingdom against kingdom, and there will be famines and earthquakes in various places. 8) All these are but the beginning of the birth pains. 9) 'Then they will deliver you up to tribulation and put you to death, and you will be hated by all nations for my name's sake. 10) And then many will fall away and betray one another and hate one another. 11) And many false prophets will arise and lead many astray. 12) And because lawlessness will be increased, the love of many will grow cold. 13) But the one who endures to the end will be saved. 14) And this gospel of the kingdom will be proclaimed throughout the whole world as a testimony to all nations, and then the end will come. 15) 'So when you see the abomination of desolation spoken of by the prophet Daniel, standing in the holy place (let the reader understand), 16) then let those who are in Judea flee to the mountains. 17) Let the one who is on the housetop not go down to take what is in his house, 18) and let the one who is in the field not turn back to take his cloak. 19) And alas for women who are pregnant and for those who are nursing infants in those days! 20) Pray that your flight may not be in winter or on a Sabbath. 21) For then there will be great tribulation, such as has not been from the beginning of the world until now, no, and never will be. 22) And if those days had not been cut short, no human being would be saved. But for the sake of the elect those days will be cut short. 23) Then if anyone says to you, 'Look, here is the Christ!' or 'There he is!' do not believe it. 24) For false christs and false prophets will arise and perform great signs and wonders, so as to lead astray, if possible, even the elect. 25) See, I have told you beforehand. 26) So, if they say to you, 'Look, he is in the wilderness,' do not go out. If they say, 'Look, he is in the inner rooms,' do not believe it. 27) For as the lightning comes from the east and shines as far as the west, so will be the coming of the Son of Man.

28) Wherever the corpse is, there the vultures will gather. 29) 'Immediately after the tribulation of those days the sun will be darkened, and the moon will not give its light, and the stars will fall from heaven, and the powers of the heavens will be shaken. 30) Then will appear in heaven the sign of the Son of Man, and then all the tribes of the earth will mourn, and they will see the Son of Man coming on the clouds of heaven with power and great glory. 31) And he will send out his angels with a loud trumpet call, and they will gather his elect from the four winds, from one end of heaven to the other. 32) 'From the fig tree learn its lesson: as soon as its branch becomes tender and puts out its leaves, you know that summer is near. 33) So also, when you see all these things, you know that he is near, at the very gates. 34) Truly, I say to you, this generation will not pass away until all these things take place. 35) Heaven and earth will pass away, but my words will not pass away.' (Mt 24:1-28).

As the disciples were leaving the temple, Jesus foretold that it would be destroyed. In response to this startling prediction about a coming time of tribulation the apostles asked Jesus two inter-related questions, firstly, when would the temple be destroyed? and secondly, when would the end times come? His response began in verse five when he said that during the time of tribulation there would be false messiahs. In his *Antiquities,* contemporary Jewish historian Josephus pointed out that there were indeed many false Messiahs between 40 and 70 AD, e.g., Theudas, Judah the Galilean, and one unnamed Egyptian Jew.[6] In verse six Jesus warned that there would be wars and rumours of wars and indeed there were. For example, in 68 AD there was widespread revolt during which

[6] Josephus, Antiquities. 20.8.6.

the emperor Nero committed suicide. In verses seven and eight Jesus spoke about the prospect of famines and earthquakes occurring. As bishop Eusebius said in his *Church History*, there was a worldwide famine at the time of the emperor, Claudius, and there were a number of others between the 50s and 60s AD. In verses nine to fourteen Jesus warned about forthcoming persecution, apostasy and evangelisation. The early followers of Jesus were persecuted by orthodox Jews (cf. Acts 7) and by gentile pagans, e.g., by the emperor Nero in the 60s.[7] As a result eleven of the twelve apostles died martyr's deaths. Revelation, chapters 1-3 attest to the fact that during that time of persecution many Christians fearing for their lives did fall away from the faith. At the same time, however, the gospel of the kingdom was proclaimed throughout the whole world within a generation. Pitre explains that two scripture verses Rm 1:6 and Col 1:5-6 indicate that phrase 'the whole world' had a restricted meaning which referred to the known Roman world as opposed to the whole non-Roman world including places like Africa, America and Asia.

When Jesus talked about the abomination of desolation in verses 15 to 28 he was referring primarily to the destruction of Jerusalem and its temple by the Romans who were pagans like King Antiochus Epiphanes who had persecuted the Jews and profaned the temple by placing a statue of a pagan god within its precincts between 175 and 164 BC. Jesus' mention of the abomination of desolation was a reference to Dan 9:26-27 which said,

> 'After the sixty-two weeks, a Messiah shall be cut off [killed], and shall have nothing; and the people of the prince who is to come shall destroy the city [Jerusalem] and the sanctuary.

---

[7] Eusebius, *Church History*.

Its end shall come with a flood; and to the end there shall be war; desolations are decreed... he shall cause sacrifice and offering to cease; and upon the wing of abominations shall come one who makes desolate.'

The desolation occurred when the pagan Romans attacked and destroyed Jerusalem and its magnificent temple. Jesus warned that when these events took place the believers should flee from Judea. As Pitre points out, this particular instruction would not be relevant in the end times, it referred specifically to the destruction of Jerusalem.

Pitre argues that rather than talking about the end times, references to the darkening of the sun, moon and stars, were borrowed from Old Testament apocalyptic writing (cf. Is 13; 34; Ezch 32). These cosmic signs were associated in the Old Testament with the destruction of cities and nations. Jesus was associating them with Jerusalem whose inhabitants were persecuting those who believed in the messiah. As a result they would suffer enormously at the hands of the Romans, as earlier Jews had suffered at the hands of the Babylonians. It was much the same where mention of 'the Son of Man coming on the clouds of heaven' was concerned. The notion of coming in that way was associated in the Old Testament with judgment on cities and territories. For instance, in Jer 14:13-14 we read,

'Behold, he [God] comes up like clouds, his chariots like the whirlwind; his horses are swifter than eagles—woe to us, for we are ruined! O Jerusalem, wash your heart from wickedness, that you may be saved.'

In his reference to the fig tree in verse thirty two Jesus was saying, that when all the events he had foretold had been fulfilled then the destruction of the temple would be close at hand. In short, Jesus was referring - not primarily to the end of *the* world - but to the end of *a* world, namely, the end of the Old Covenant as embodied by the city of Jerusalem and the Temple.

THE PREDICTION OF JESUS WAS FULFILLED

In his book, *Jesus Before Christianity*, Dominican author Albert Nolan argued that all through his public ministry, Jesus, like John the Baptist before him, had a sense of an impending and unprecedented disaster (cf. Lk 19:43-44; 21:20-24).[8] He told the people that catastrophe could be avoided if they accepted Jesus and responded with faith and repentance to his good news proclamation. However, as his public ministry drew to its end it was quite apparent to Jesus that, by and large, the people were not responding to his Good News message. As a result we are told that he declared with tears in his eyes, 'O Jerusalem, Jerusalem, you who kill the prophets and stone those sent to you, how often I have longed to gather your children together, as a hen gathers her chicks under her wings, but you were not willing. Look, your house is left to you desolate' (Mt 23:37-39).

The warning and prediction of Jesus were fulfilled a generation or so after his death and resurrection. Writing around the year 115 AD, Roman historian Tacitus said that in 66 A.D., shortly before the destruction of the temple there were ominous signs, at Pentecost time, of what was about to happen. He wrote, 'A sudden lightning flash from the clouds lit up the Temple. The doors of the holy place abruptly opened, a superhuman voice was heard to declare that the

---

[8] (London: Darton, Longman & Todd, 1992), 5-23.

gods were leaving it, and at the same instant came the rushing tumult of their departure.' There is an account of a similar phenomenon in 2 Macc 5:2-4. The citizens of Jerusalem were being fiercely persecuted by pagan king Antiochus IV. We are told that, 'It then happened that all over the city, for nearly forty days, there appeared horsemen, clothed in garments of a golden weave, charging in mid-air - companies fully armed with lances and drawn swords; squadrons of cavalry in battle array, charges and counter charges on this side and that, with brandished shields and bristling spears, flights of arrows and flashes of gold ornaments, together with armour of every sort.' Shortly afterwards the citizens of Jerusalem were slaughtered.

The temple had lost its meaning as a unique locus of encounter between God and humans and had been replaced by the living temple, namely the Christian community which is the Body of Christ on earth. The temple sacrifices for the forgiveness of sins had ended and had been replaced by the once only, all-sufficient sacrifice of Jesus on the cross. The Jewish priesthood was largely redundant and replaced by Christ, the eternal high priest. As Jesus had said to the Samaritan woman at the well of Samaria, 'You worship what you do not know; we worship what we know, for salvation is from the Jews. But the hour is coming, and is now here, when the true worshipers will worship the Father in spirit and truth' (Jn 4:22-3).

Between 132-36 AD there was another Jewish uprising which was led by a messianic figure called Simon bar Kokhba. It was put down in a merciless way by the Romans. Deaths resulting from that war are estimated to be 580,000 Jews and hundreds of thousands of Romans. Following the Roman victory, Jewish settlements were not rebuilt and many of the survivors were sold into slavery in Egypt. Jerusalem was renamed Aelia Capitolina and Jews were once again banned from living there. So for nearly 2,000 years Jerusalem has been a Gentile city. However, as has been noted already, possibly one of the signs of the beginning of the end times became apparent when Israel became a country and West Jerusalem was nominated its capital in June 1967.

It is significant that the Christians had neither defended the temple or the city between 66 and 70 AD, nor got involved in the Simon bar Kokhba revolt between 132 and 136 AD. It was probably due to the fact that they wanted to abide by the teaching of Jesus in Mt 24:16-21. Mindful of Our Lord's prophecy, the Christian believers had left the city for Pella in Trans-Jordan during the first Jewish war. According to the Christian historian Eusebius they decided to flee the city after a command to do so had been communicated to 'those who were worthy' by a revelation.

There is an interesting addendum to this story. In 130 AD the Roman Emperor Hadrian visited the ruins of the Jewish Temple in Jerusalem. Although he promised to rebuild the Temple, the Jews felt betrayed when they found out that he intended to build a pagan temple dedicated to Jupiter. Years later in 361 AD Julian the Apostate, a nephew of the emperor Constantine, decided to help the Jews to rebuild the temple in Jerusalem so that animal sacrifices could once more be offered there. It is thought that he was motivated by a desire to prove that the prophecies of Daniel and Jesus were false. All this happened while Saint Cyril (c. 313 – 386 AD) was Bishop of Jerusalem. Even though Julian employed the power and resources of the empire, and the Jews helped him with generous financial contributions and practical help, it is said that

Cyril was unmoved. 'The word of God abides,' he is reported to have said; 'one stone will not be laid on another.'[9]

When the building project got going the rubble was cleared away and the foundations laid bare, but then there was an earthquake that killed and maimed many workers. When the work recommenced, the historian Ammianus Marcellinus (c.330 – 395 AD) tells us in his *'Res Gestae,'* book 23 that, 'terrible balls of fire kept bursting forth near the foundations of the Temple and made the place inaccessible to the workmen, some of whom were burned to death.'[10] Another historian called Sozomen (c.375-447 AD) recounted in his *Ecclesiastical History,* book 5, chapter 22 that, 'A more tangible and still more extraordinary prodigy ensued; suddenly the sign of the cross appeared spontaneously on the garments of the persons engaged in the undertaking. These crosses were disposed like stars, and appeared the work of art. Many were led to confess that Christ is God, and that the rebuilding of the temple was not pleasing to Him; others presented themselves in the church, were initiated, and besought Christ, with hymns and supplications, to pardon their transgression.'

Some people think that there is reason to believe that a third temple will be rebuilt before the end times and that it will be connected with the anti-Christ figure mentioned by Paul in 2 Theses 2:4, as 'taking his seat in the very temple of God.' Although this phrase could be understood in a symbolic way, it could also be a prophetic reference to the building of a third temple. Apparently, the Temple

---

[9] *Catechetical Lectures,* no. 15, par. 15.

[10] Some people hypothesise that methane gas which was trapped in the still existing underground section of the former temple suddenly escaped and ignited.

Institute in modern day Jerusalem has released a contemporary three-dimensional architectural representation of the future Third Holy Temple, utilising the latest building materials and techniques. The Institute has also recreated over 70 sacred vessels for use in the Temple. They can be seen at a Visitor's Centre in the Old City of Jerusalem. So if a time comes when the Israelis announce that they are going to rebuild the temple it could be a sure sign that the end times are imminent. Meantime the destruction of Jerusalem and its temple in 70 A.D. prefigured, in a symbolic way, the much greater cosmic disaster that will precede the second coming of Jesus Christ.

SIGNIFICANCE OF THE DESTRUCTION OF THE TEMPLE

Scripture scholars such as Brant Pitre and N T Wright say that there was great apocalyptic significance in the destruction of the temple. For the Jews it was not just a building, it was a microcosm of the universe. That linkage is evident in Ps 78:69 which says, 'He built his sanctuary [temple] like the high heavens, like the earth, which he has founded forever.' In his book , *The Temple*, G. K. Beale quotes the words of a second century rabbi who said, 'The house of the Holy of Holies is made to correspond to the highest heaven. The outer holy house was made to correspond to the earth. And the courtyard was made to correspond to the sea.'[11] Beale also mentions other aspects of the temple which had cosmic significance such as Seven Lamps of the Menorah which symbolised the seven (visible) planets; the curtains which were coloured blue and purple which represented the heavens; and the Outer Veil, which had the 'panorama of the heavens' portrayed on it. In the temple heaven touched the earth. As Jacob said at the shrine in Bethel, 'Truly, the

---

[11] *The Temple and the Church's Mission: A Biblical Theology of the Dwelling Place of God* (Wheaton: IVP, 2004), 46 n. 36.

Lord is in this spot, although I did not know it!' In solemn wonder he cried out: 'How awesome is this shrine! This is nothing else but an abode of God, and that is the gateway to heaven!' (Gen 28: 16-17).

So when the temple was completely destroyed it was symbolic in apocalyptic terms of the end of heaven and earth. So one can say that although Jesus was not primarily talking about the end of the world when he spoke about the impending destruction of the temple, he did see it as a harbinger of the greater cosmic tribulation which would precede his second coming, the final judgement and the symbolic re-establishment of God's spiritual temple in a transformed cosmos.

In the Olivet discourse, Jesus said in verse eight that all he had described was merely, 'the beginning of birth pains' which would eventually bring forth new life in his second coming. In the meantime we live in the period of on-going labour pain, so to speak, when all the things that Jesus mentioned in his Olivet discourse will recur in different ways during the centuries that elapse between his two advents.

1)   We always have had wars and rumours of wars. Milton Leitenberg has estimated that 130–142 million military and civilian deaths occurred as a result of war and conflicts during the 20th century. It was the bloodiest hundred years in human history. Apparently, before the world's end there will be an even more brutal and deadly conflagration.

2)   Earthquakes too, have been a constant feature down the years. For instance, the great Chilean earthquake of 1960 was measured at 9.5 on the Richter Scale. It left two million people

homeless and created a tsunami which crossed the Pacific Ocean at two hundred miles an hour. Even more devastating earthquakes could occur in the future.

3)   Throughout its history different regions of the world have experienced famines. For example, in Europe there was the Great Famine of 1315-17, during which between 10% and 25% of the population died. In more recent times there have been famines in various parts of the world, e.g., in Ethiopia in 1984 and Yemen in 2019.

4)   There have also been great outbreaks of pestilence throughout history such as the black death which resulted in the death of an estimated 75 to 200 million people between 1347 to 1351. The 1918 influenza pandemic, known as the Spanish flu, resulted in the deaths of anything between 50 and 100 million people.

5)   From the earliest years Christians have been persecuted, notably during the reign of the Roman Emperor Nero. At a conference in Rome in 2014, Pope Francis said that he was 'greatly pained to note that Christians around the world are suffering the greatest discrimination. The persecution of Christians today is even greater than in the first centuries of the Church, and there are more Christian martyrs today than in that era.'

Just as the events that occurred between the ascension of Jesus and the Jewish war, were intimations of the destruction of the temple in 70 A.D., so too the disasters that have punctuated the pages of human history presage great tribulation which is yet to come.

POSSIBLE SIGNIFICANCE OF THE FIG TREE
We have already adverted to the fact that in Mt 24:32-35 Jesus said,

'Now learn this lesson from the fig tree: As soon as its twigs get tender and its leaves come out, you know that summer is near. Even so, when you see all these things, you know that it is near, right at the door. I tell you the truth, this generation will certainly not pass away until all these things have happened. Heaven and earth will pass away, but my words will never pass away.' The destruction of Jerusalem and the temple together with its violent aftermath marked the end of the Jewish nation and led to the dispersal of its people all over the world for a period of 1,800 years or so.

However, the Old Testament seemed to foretell that the nation would be re-established in a day. In Is 66:8 we read, 'Shall a land be born in one day? Shall a nation be brought forth in one moment?' In Ezek 36:35-36, we read, 'this land that was laid waste has become like the garden of Eden; the cities that were lying in ruins, desolate and destroyed, are now fortified and inhabited.' Then the nations around you that remain will know that I the Lord have rebuilt what was destroyed and have replanted what was desolate. I the Lord have spoken, and I will do it.' Some Christians maintain that those prophecies were fulfilled in 1948 when the state of Israel came into being along with its ancient language and traditions. Speaking about this phenomenon, a footnote in the *Amplified Bible*, says, 'Never in the history of the world had such a thing happened before – but God keeps his word. As definitely foretold by Isaiah and Ezekiel, Israel became a recognised nation, actually 'born in one day.' Commenting on these significant events Papal preacher Raniero Cantalamessa wrote,

'Can we Christians exclude that what is happening in our day, that is, the return of Israel to the land of its fathers, is not connected in some way, still a mystery to us, to this providential order which concerns the chosen people and which is carried out even through human error and excess as happens in the Church itself? If Israel is to enter the New Covenant one day, St. Paul tells us that they will not do so a few at a time but as an entire nation, as ever-living 'roots.' But if Israel is to enter as a nation, it must be a nation; it must have a land of its own, an organisation and a voice in the midst of other nations of the earth. The fact that Israel has remained an ethnic unity throughout the centuries and throughout many historical upheavals is, in itself, a sign of a destiny that has not been interrupted but is waiting to be fulfilled.'[12]

The fig tree, which is understood by many as a metaphor for Israel has been animated by new life in recent years. According to some scholars, Jesus regarded this as a harbinger of the immanence of the end times. So when he said that, 'I tell you the truth, this generation will certainly not pass away until all these things have happened' (Mt 24:34), as well as referring to the people who were listening to him during his lifetime, many of whom lived to witness the destruction of Jerusalem and the temple, he might also have been referring to the people who would be living when the Jewish state came into existences either in 1948 when it was established by the United Nations or in 2018 when the Jewish Knesset passed a law which asserted two main things. Firstly, the ability to exercise national self-determination in Israel is the sole right of the Jewish people. Secondly, the ancient language of Hebrew was established as the official language of the country.

Ever since 1948 Jews from all the tribes of Israel have been returning

---

[12] *The Mystery of Christmas* (Middlegreen: St Paul Publications, 1988), 99.

to their native land. In recent years, even Jews from the lost tribes have come back. For example, in North East India, there is a small group of people who have been practicing Judaism for more than 27 years. They believe that they have rediscovered the religion of their ancestors. They call themselves Bnei Menashe (or Manmaseh), and believe that they are descendants of the Tribe of Menashe, one of the ten lost tribes.[13] They understand their history of exile from the Northern Kingdom of Israel in 721 B.C. as a result of travelling the silk route and finally ending up in India and Myanmar (Burma). In recent years hundreds of them have emigrated to Israel. Our Lord's words about the fig tree could be understood in such a way as to imply that within a generation after 1948 or 2018, the end times would be inaugurated, i.e., in the near rather than the distant future. Time will tell. While it is an interesting hypothesis, I'm sceptical about this particular interpretation of the meaning of Mt 24:32. One way or the other we have to recall the words of Jesus in Mt 24:36, 'But about that day or hour no one knows, not even the angels in heaven, nor the Son, but only the Father.'

CONCLUSION

When one reads through the statements Jesus made about the end times, they are rather general. As we know there have been such things as the wars, earthquakes, and famines he referred to right down the centuries, but none of them, as yet, has inaugurated the second coming. Presumably, such phenomena will be heightened in intensity before the end of history, but it would seem that we will not be able to judge when the precise end has come until it suddenly springs upon us like a bear trap that has been unexpectedly triggered into action. We can conclude this chapter with some words spoken by St John Paul II.

---

[13] Roy Schoeman, Salvation is From the Jews (San Francisco: Ignatius, 2003), 308.

'We know that the apocalyptic images of the eschatological discourse about the end of all things should be interpreted in the light of their intense symbolism. They express the precariousness of the world and the sovereign power of Christ, in whose hands has been placed the destiny of humanity. History advances towards its goal, but Christ has not specified any chronological date. Attempts to predict the end of the world are therefore deceptive and misleading. Christ has assured us only that the end will not come before his saving work has reached a universal dimension through the preaching of the Gospel: 'This Gospel of the kingdom will be preached throughout the whole world, as a testimony to all nations; and then the end will come' (Mt 24:14).'[14]

---

[14] Par 3 of *Christ's Final Coming* - At the General Audience of Wednesday, April 22, 1998. http://www.vatican.va/jubilee_2000/magazine/documents/ju_mag_01101998_p-27_en.html

FOUR

ST. PAUL AND THE END-TIMES

SOME SCHOLARS ARGUE, WITH A DEGREE OF JUSTIFICATION, that while Jesus was the founder of Christianity, St Paul was the one who best interpreted and promulgated the meaning and significance of his life death and resurrection. One amazing thing about Paul is the fact that he didn't seem to be taught about Jesus. By his own admission, everything was revealed to him. He testified, 'the gospel that was preached by me is not man's gospel. For I did not receive it from any man, nor was I taught it, but I received it through a revelation of Jesus Christ . . . (he) who called me by his grace, was pleased to reveal his Son to me, in order that I might preach him among the Gentiles' (Gal 1:12; 15). That kind of revelation is prophetic in the sense that it was given to Paul in a supernatural way. This is worth mentioning because when Paul was asked about the end times his responses were not the product of his own theological thinking, but rather the result of having received revelation from God.

Due to a misunderstanding of the teaching of Jesus about the destruction of the temple in Jerusalem and the end times, many of the early Christians seem to have expected the second coming to occur within their lifetimes during the first century AD. It would appear that early in his career St Paul may have shared that belief. For example, in 1 Thess 4:16-17, which was probably the first inspired scripture to be written in the New Testament around 52 AD, he said,

'For the Lord himself will descend from heaven with a cry of command, with the voice of an archangel, and with the sound of the trumpet of God. And the dead in Christ will rise first. Then we who are alive, who are left, will be caught up together with them in the clouds to meet the Lord in the air, and so we will always be with the Lord. Therefore encourage one another with these words.'

The phrase, 'we who are alive' may have implied that Paul thought that he would be still alive when the second coming of Jesus took place. By the time he wrote his second letter to the Thessalonians, however, Paul made it clear that he didn't think that the *parousia* was immanent. Apparently some of the Christians in Thessalonica had come to believe, perhaps as a result of a prophecy or a letter purporting to have come from Paul, that the end times had already begun.

In 2 Thess 2:3-4, he explained,

'Let no one in any way deceive you, for that day cannot come without the coming of the apostasy first, and the appearing of the man of sin, the son of perdition, who sets himself against, and exalts himself above, every so-called `god' or object of worship, and goes the length of taking his seat in the very temple of God, giving it out that he himself is God.'

What Paul was indicating was the fact that a number of important things would have to happen before Jesus' return. As Cardinal John Newman said, 'As long as the world lasts, this passage of Scripture will be full of reverent interest to Christians. It is their duty ever to be watching for the advent of their Lord, to search for the signs of it in all that happens around them; and above all to keep in mind this great and awful sign of which St. Paul speaks to the Thessalonians.'[1] At this point we will take a closer look at what he said while examining some of its possible implications.

A] THE GREAT APOSTASY

Paul predicted that there would be a great apostasy before the end times. The word apostasy is derived from Greek and means to rebel or to defect. Christian apostates are those who fall away, in a theoretical or practical sense, by rejecting the beliefs and morals of Christ and his church. Apostasy, therefore is the opposite of conversion; it is de-conversion. There is nothing new about this phenomenon. It seems to be evident in two stories recounted in the post resurrection gospel accounts. Firstly, there is the description of the two disciples on the road to Emmaus. Surely there was symbolic significance in the fact that they were travelling away from Jerusalem (cf. Lk 24:13–35). In other words they seemed to have abandoned any hope they had invested in Jesus and the coming of his kingdom. Secondly, although Jesus had appeared to the apostles after his resurrection, Peter said to his companions, 'I'm going fishing.' Immediately a number of them decided to join him. In other words, because of their disillusionment with Jesus, they may have been intending to forget about him and to go back to their old way of life as skilful, experienced fishermen (cf. Jn 21: 1-14).[2]

---

[1] John Henry Cardinal Newman. Lecture 1. 'The Times of Antichrist' in The Patristical Idea of Antichrist in Four Lectures, in *Discussions and Arguments on Various Subjects* (London: Pickering, 1872).

[2] Cf. John Marsh, Saint John: *The Pelican Gospel Commentaries* (London: Penguin Books, 1968), 658.

Saint Paul wrote about this phenomenon in 1 Tim 4:1-2, 'The Spirit clearly says that in later times some will abandon the faith and follow deceiving spirits and things taught by demons. Such teachings come through hypocritical liars, whose consciences have been seared as with a hot iron.' The expression 'in later times' is not as strong as the phrase 'in the last days' (2 Tim 3:1). Evidently, the conditions Paul discusses here were taking place during his lifetime. Centuries later St. Thomas Aquinas observed, 'A person may apostatise from God, by rebelling in his or her mind against the Divine commandments: and though a person may apostatise . . . he or she may still remain united to God by faith.'[3]

While it is true that apostasy has occurred on many occasions over the centuries, e.g., Gnosticism in the early Church, Catharism between the 12th and 14th centuries, and the French Revolution in the 18th century, it could be argued that the apostasy that is currently taking place in the developed countries of the Western world is unprecedented in its scale. St John Henry Newman was aware of it in the 19th century. He wrote,

'There are evidences to convince us that we are entering the Age of Apostasy. For apostasy is being formed, gathering force, gaining ground on the Christian Church every day. Everywhere in the world, but quite visibly in the most peaceful, civilised nations, we are witnessing a supreme effort to govern people and dominate the world without religion . . . In almost every country there is a united, powerful movement to crush the Church, to strip her of power and place.'[4]

---

[3] St Thomas Aquinas, *Summa Theologiae: A Concise Translation*, ed. Timothy McDermott (London: Methuen, 1989), 343.

[4] 'Advent Sermons on the Antichrist' in *Tracts for Out Times* (London: Rivington,

I was interested to see that Newman quoted a remarkable extract from a letter which was written in 1834 by a Bishop Horsley of Rochester. He was well versed in physics and mathematics. In the light of subsequent events in contemporary Europe what he said about modern apostasy sounds extraordinarily prescient.

'The Church of God on earth will be greatly reduced, as we may well imagine, in its apparent numbers, in the times of Antichrist, by the open desertion of the powers of the world. This desertion will begin in a professed indifference to any particular form of Christianity, under the pretence of universal toleration; which toleration will proceed from no true spirit of charity and forbearance, but from a design to undermine Christianity . . . The pretended toleration will go far beyond a just toleration, even as it regards the different sects of Christians. For governments will pretend an indifference to all, and will give a protection in preference to none. All establishments will be laid aside. From the toleration of the most pestilent heresies, they will proceed to the toleration of Islam, Atheism, and at last to a positive persecution of the truth of Christianity. In these times the Temple of God will be reduced almost to the Holy Place, that is, to the small number of real Christians who worship the Father in spirit and in truth, and regulate their doctrine and their worship, and their whole conduct, strictly by the word of God. The merely nominal Christians will all desert the profession of the truth, when the powers of the world desert it. . . . The property of the clergy will be pillaged, the public worship insulted and vilified by these deserters of the faith they once professed, who are not called apostates because they never were in

1840), 12.

earnest in their profession. Their profession was nothing more than a compliance with fashion and public authority. In principle they were always, what they now appear to be, Gentiles. When this general desertion of the faith takes place, then will commence the sackcloth ministry of the witnesses ... There will be nothing of splendour in the external appearance of their churches; they will have no support from governments, no honours, no emoluments, no immunities, no authority, but that which no earthly power can take away, which they derived from Him, who commissioned them to be His witnesses.'[5]

In the mid 20th century St John XXIII said in his encyclical, *Aeterna Dei Sapientia* (God's Eternal Wisdom), pars. 70-71,

'Venerable Brethren, the fifteenth centenary of the death of St. Leo the Great finds the Catholic Church in much the same plight as she was at the turn of the fifth century. The same waves of bitter hostility break upon her. How many violent storms does she not enter in these days of ours - storms which trouble Our fatherly heart, even though our Divine Redeemer clearly forewarned us of them! On every side we see 'the faith of the gospel' imperilled. In some quarters an attempt is being made - usually to no avail - to induce bishops, priests and faithful to withdraw their allegiance from this See of Rome, the stronghold of Catholic unity.'

---

[5] John Henry Cardinal Newman. 'The Patristical Idea of Antichrist in Four Lectures' in *Discussions and Arguments on Various Subjects* (London: Pickering, 1872). These views found an echo in a radio talk of Joseph Ratzinger (Pope Benedict XVI) on German radio. See Pat Collins, C.M., *Prophesy: Truth for Today, Light for Tomorrow* (Luton: New Life, 2018), 142-4.

John Paul II said in par. 9 of *Ecclesia in Europa* (The Church in Europe),

> 'European culture gives the impression of 'silent apostasy' on the part of people who have all that they need and who live as if God does not exist.'[6]

G. K. Chesterton once pointed out that, 'when people cease to believe in God they do not go on to believe in nothing; they then become capable of believing anything.' I have found in Britain and Ireland that as people drift away from orthodox Christian belief, they begin to become involved in all kinds of occult and New Age ideas together with superstitious practices such as astrology, palmistry, spiritualism, Reiki, kundalini, fortune telling, contacting the dead, consulting mediums, and using Ouija boards or tarot cards in a misguided effort to contact the world of spirits or to gain control over their lives and their futures. In engaging in these and similar activities, people can unwittingly open themselves to the influence of evil spirits as Paul said in 2 Tim 3:1. Whether the apostasy we are witnessing at present is the beginning of the rebellion predicted by Paul remains to be seen, but it is certainly an intimation of what will happen on a wide scale before the end times.

---

[6] For example, in a recent 2019 survey in Britain only 3% of adults under 24 described themselves as Anglican and fewer than the 5% who identified as Catholic. Almost three out of four 18 to 24 year-olds said they had no religion, a rise of nine percentage points since 2015. More generally, 53% of all adults described themselves as having no religious affiliation, up from 48% in 2015. Roger Harding, of the National Centre for Social Research which published the survey, said the latest figures followed 'the long-term trend of more and more of us not being religious.'

B] *THE MAN OF LAWLESSNESS*

Paul says that before Christ's return, a mysterious antichrist figure will set himself up in opposition to God. Antichrist is a name that is used in three New Testament texts. The first is in 1 Jn 2:18, 'Children, it is the last hour; and just as you heard that the antichrist was coming, so now many antichrists have appeared.' The second is in 1 Jn 4:3, 'Every spirit which does not confess Jesus is not of God. This is the spirit of Antichrist, of which you heard that it was coming, and now it is in the world already.' The third is in 2 Jn 1:7, 'For many deceivers have gone out into the world, men who will not acknowledge the coming of Jesus Christ in the flesh; such a one is a deceiver and the Antichrist.' In the early Church a number of evil people were said to be Antichrists, such as Antiochus, Nero, Domitian, and Julian the apostate. Preaching on the letters of St John, St Augustine identified the Antichrist with heretics and schismatics who broke faith with the true Church. He went on to also speak of Antichrists who remain in the Church – those who confess Christ with their mouths while denying him with their deeds.

St. Robert Bellarmine, S.J., (1542-1621), a doctor of the Church, wrote, 'The name 'Antichrist' . . . means someone contrary to Christ; not contrary in any way whatever, but so much so that he will fight against that which pertains to the seat and dignity of Christ; that is, one who will be a rival of Christ and to be held as Christ, after he who truly is Christ has been cast out.'[7] Bellarmine also pointed out that on some occasions the term Antichrist refers to 'a certain distinct enemy of Christ' and sometimes it refers to 'all who oppose

---

[7] *Antichrist* (Post Falls, ID: Mediatrix Press, 2016), 5. See also, Joseph L. Iannuzzi. *Antichrist and the End Times* (McKees Rocks, PA: St Andrew's Productions, 2005), 99.

Christ.' Commenting on the term Antichrist, twentieth century theologians Karl Rahner and Herbert Vorgrimler wrote, 'It is possible to understand the statements of Scripture as meaning that the Antichrist is the embodiment of all those historical forces hostile to God which are under the control of man.'[8] It can also refer to one particular human being who will be the definitive Antichrist because he will personify all that is evil. He will be the antithesis of the divine holiness of Jesus. In 2 Cor 11:14, St Paul warns believers that 'Satan himself masquerades as an angel of light.' So when the antichrist appears, he will probably be attractive, impressive and a wonder worker who will seduce and deceive the majority of the people, much as Hitler did in Germany.

There is a great deal of evidence that evil, although it is pervasive in modern society is not always recognised for what it is. For instance in par. 80 of his encyclical *Veritatis Splendor* (Splendour of the Truth), St. John Paul II wrote that the,

> 'Second Vatican Council itself, in discussing the respect due to the human person, cited a number of examples of intrinsically evil acts: 'Whatever is hostile to life itself, such as any kind of homicide, genocide, abortion, euthanasia and voluntary suicide; whatever violates the integrity of the human person, such as mutilation, physical and mental torture and attempts to coerce the spirit; whatever is offensive to human dignity, such as sub-human living conditions, arbitrary imprisonment, deportation, slavery, prostitution and trafficking in women and children; degrading conditions of work which treat labourers as mere instruments of profit, and not as free responsible persons: all

---

[8] *Theological Dictionary* (New York: Herder &Herder, 1968), 28-29.

ST. PAUL AND THE END-TIMES

these and the like are a disgrace, and so long as they infect human civilisation they contaminate those who inflict them more than those who suffer injustice, and they are a negation of the honour due to the Creator.'

Sadly, all of those forms of intrinsic evil are evident in the world today. While I do believe that we are entering the final confrontation, spoken about by John Paul II,[9] that doesn't necessarily mean that the end times that St. Paul had in mind in 2 Thess 2:3-4 are imminent.

THE ANTICHRIST AND A FALSE MESSIANISM

The Antichrist[10] figure that Paul mentions will be a messianic type person, perhaps a Jew from the tribe of Dan, with his or her own brand of messianism. For a couple of centuries now we have been experiencing an anticipatory form of pseudo messianism whereby man glorifies himself in the place of God. For instance, philosopher, Ludwig Feuerbach (1804-1872), a former Protestant was a proponent of this kind of world view. He wrote an influential book *The Essence of Christianity*, in which he stated, 'God did not, as the Bible says, make man in His image; on the contrary man, as I have shown in *The Essence of Christianity*, made God in his image.'[11] He argued that all statements about God, are in fact, statements about human beings and their potential. He also wrote, 'The task of the modern era was the realisation and humanisation of God – the

---

[9] Cf. Pat Collins, C.M., *Prophesy: Truth for Today, Light for Tomorrow* (Luton: New Life, 2018), 145-6.

[10] Cf. Joseph L. Iannuzzi, *Antichrist and the End Times* (McKees Rocks, PA: St Andrew's Productions, 2005).

[11] Lecture XX, in *Lectures on the Essence of Religion* (New York: Harper & Row. 1967), 187

transformation and dissolution of theology into anthropology.'[12] He added, 'God is merely the projected essence of man. What therefore, ranks second in religion – namely, Man – that must be proclaimed the first and recognised as the first. If the nature of Man is man's highest being, if to be human is his highest existence, then man's love for man, must in practice become the first and highest law. Man's God is man. This is the highest law of ethics. This is the turning point of world history.'[13]

That viewpoint was implicit during the French Revolution when churches across France were transformed into modern Temples of Reason. The most outstanding example of all was at the cathedral of Notre Dame in Paris. The Christian altar was dismantled and an altar to Liberty was installed and the inscription 'To Philosophy' was carved in stone over the cathedral's doors. An actress called Sophie Momoro was enthroned, in a blasphemous way, as the goddess of reason. Feuerbach has had a big influence upon many Western thinkers. As Pope John Paul II pointed out in par. 9 of *Ecclesia in Europa* (The Church in Europe), a purely humanistic understanding of human beings is widespread in contemporary secular society.

Besides this form of humanism there was the socio-political version of Karl Marx. Communism was, and still is, an example. It denies the existence of God while it strives, by human effort alone, to create a heaven here on earth. Emile Durkheim (1858-1917) the father of the sociology of religion argued that 'god and society are

---

[12] Ludwig. Feuerbach, *Principles of the Philosophy of the Future* (Indianapolis, Hackett Publishing Company, 1986), 5.

[13] Ludwig Feuerbach, *The Essence of Christianity* (New York: Frederick Ungar Publishing Co. , 1957), 65.

one of the same...the god of the clan...can be none other than the clan itself.'[14] Speaking about Feuerbach, Sigmund Freud (1856-1939) the originator of psychoanalysis, said, 'Among all philosophers, I worship and admire this man the most.'[15] He summed up his mentor's position succinctly: 'religious ideas, which are given out as teachings...are illusions, fulfilments of the oldest, strongest, and most urgent wishes of mankind.'[16] Freud argued in psychological terms that God was nothing other than the projection of a childlike need for a protective, otherworldly father figure.

In capitalist countries people rely in an analogous way on the inevitability of evolutionary progress by means of such things as science, engineering, technology and capitalism which strive to create a man made utopia here on earth. In many ways psychology has become a substitute for religion in Western capitalist societies. Professor Paul Vitz, a convert to Catholicism, has stated that modern psychologists such as Erich Fromm, Carl Rogers, and Rollo May have tried to replace traditional notions of belief, with a self-glorifying humanism.[17] For example, Abraham Maslow wrote: 'I sometimes think that the world will either be saved by psychologists – in the very broadest sense – or else it will not be saved at all.'[18]

---

[14] Emile Durkheim, Elementary Forms of Religious Life (New York: Free Press, 1995), 208.

[15] Peter Gay Freud: *A Life for our Time,* p. 28)

[16] *The Future of an Illusion* (New York: W. W. Norton and Company. 1960), 30.

[17] Paul Vitz,. *Psychology as Religion : the Cult of Self-worship.* Grand Rapids: Eerdmans.1977.

[18] Speech delivered at Nebraska Convention Jan 13-14th 1955, quoted in *The Right to be Human: A Biography of Abraham Maslow* (Wellingborough: Crucible, 1989), 207.

In par. 38 of his encyclical *Lord and Giver of Life*, St John Paul II wrote in a perceptive way,

> 'The analysis of sin in its original dimension indicates that, through the influence of the 'father of lies', throughout the history of humanity there will be a constant pressure on man to reject God, even to the point of hating him: 'Love of self to the point of contempt for God,' as Saint Augustine puts it. Man will be inclined to see in God primarily a limitation of himself, and not the source of his own freedom and the fullness of good. We see this confirmed in the modern age, when the atheistic ideologies seek to root out religion on the grounds that religion causes the radical 'alienation' of man, as if man were dispossessed of his own humanity when, accepting the idea of God, he attributes to God what belongs to man, and exclusively to man! Hence a process of thought and historico-sociological practice in which the rejection of God has reached the point of declaring his 'death.'

It is striking that Pope John Paul II says that ultimately modern atheism which declares the death of God is diabolical in origin. It has many prominent advocates, men such as Richard Dawkins, Stephen Pinker, Christopher Hitchens, Stephen Hawking, Stephen Weinberg, and Daniel Dennett. So it is not surprising therefore that par. 676 of the *Catechism of the Catholic Church* says, 'The Antichrist's deception already begins to take shape in the world every time the claim is made to realise within history that messianic hope which can only be realised beyond history through the eschatological judgement. The Church has rejected even modified forms of this falsification of the kingdom to come under the name of millenarianism, especially the 'intrinsically perverse' political form of a secular messianism.'

In 2 Thess 2:6-8, Paul says,

> 'You know what is restraining him [the devil] now so that he
> may be revealed in his time. For the mystery of lawlessness
> is already at work. Only he who now restrains it will do so
> until he is out of the way. And then the lawless one will be
> revealed, whom the Lord Jesus will kill with the breath of
> his mouth and bring to nothing by the appearance of his
> coming.'

When one reads commentaries on these verses it becomes apparent
that there is no consensus about their precise meaning. As *The
New International Version Cultural Backgrounds Study Bible* says,
'views of the meaning of the restrainer include the finished
proclamation of the gospel; the presence of Christians in Jerusalem;
God's restraining hand or presence; or the archangel Michael
who is the angelic protector of Israel.'[19] However one understands
the notion of diabolical evil being restrained, its presence is not
recognised at present by the ungodly, but it will be revealed to them
in the end times and will only be overcome in a definitive way by
the breath of the Lord's mouth, a verse that seems to be derived
from Is 11:4 which says, 'he shall strike the earth with the rod of his
mouth, and with the breath of his lips he shall kill the wicked.'

In the light of these points, it is not surprising that par. 675 of the
Catechism of the Catholic Church, reflects the teaching of Jesus and
Paul when it says,

> 'Before Christ's second coming the Church must pass through
> a final trial that will shake the faith of many believers. The

---

persecution that accompanies her pilgrimage on earth will unveil the 'mystery of iniquity' in the form of a religious deception offering men an apparent solution to their problems at the price of apostasy from the truth. The supreme religious deception is that of the Antichrist, a pseudo-messianism by which man glorifies himself in place of God and of his Messiah come in the flesh.'

What is implied here is the fact that the Godless messianisms which are current in the contemporary world are a sort of down payment for what is to come in a much more severe way at the end of time. We could ask the question, is there any evidence to indicate that Paul's signposts to the end times have yet been passed?

EVANGELISATION OF THE GENTILES

In the preceding chapter we noted how Jesus said in Mt 25:14, 'And this gospel of the kingdom will be preached throughout the whole world, as a testimony to all nations; and then the end will come.' While those words were primarily about the coming destruction of Jerusalem and the temple, indirectly they intimated that before the end times the gospel would not only have been preached in all of the known world, i.e., the Roman empire, it would also have been preached to the peoples of the whole earth. In his reference to the fig tree in Romans eleven, Paul implied that God's permissive providence was at work when the majority of the Jews in the first century and afterwards rejected the good news message of Jesus as Lord and Saviour. As a result, the early Christians, notably St Paul, were able then and ever since to evangelise the Gentiles. It is arguable that as a result of worldwide missions and the pervasive influence of different forms of electronic and print media people in all parts of the world have had an opportunity of hearing about

Jesus and his saving message. However, Paul implies that when that process has been accomplished worldwide, the Jewish people will finally respond to the Gospel and so be grafted into the vine once more. As Paul said in Rm 11:24, 'if you were cut from what is by nature a wild olive tree, and grafted, contrary to nature, into a cultivated olive tree, how much more will these, the natural branches, be grafted back into their own olive tree.'

THE JEWS AND CHRIST'S RETURN

A few years ago I spoke at a conference at Skalka in the Slovak Republic. Each evening I travelled to my lodgings which were in a school. I noticed that next to where I was staying was a large and impressive Jewish synagogue. When I enquired about it, I was told that there were no Jews remaining in the area and that the synagogue was now an art gallery. When I asked where the Jews had gone, the locals said in a vague generalised way that they had left during World War II. However, when I walked around the building I noticed a reference to many members of the congregation who had been killed. Subsequently I discovered that 105,000 Slovak Jews had died during the war. It seemed to me that the non Jewish Slovaks were in denial as far as these statistics were concerned.

On one of the days during the conference, I said quite spontaneously that I had been moved by the fate of the Trencin Jews and had an intention of praying outside the Synagogue for all the members of the congregation who had been executed. I said that if anyone was interested they could join me the following day. When the meeting ended quite a number of people said they would like to join me in praying for the Jews. One of the men said he knew a woman who had the keys of the synagogue and would try to have it opened when we arrived. In the event about forty adults and teenagers turned up. We were admitted to the beautiful building. Inside we found that the floor space had been prepared for an exhibition of Christian iconography. It was ironic to say the least because during the pro-Nazi regime of President Jozef Tiso, a Catholic priest, it was agreed to deport Slovak Jews as part of the Nazi Final Solution.[20] We went up the stairs to a gallery where we read passages from Paul's letter to the Romans chapters 9 and 11, prayed, and sang hymns. It was a profoundly emotional experience that moved many people to tears. When we left the synagogue a psychiatrist told me that she intended to go to the bishop to talk about the necessity of praying for the Jews. A priest told me he intended to visit a Messianic Jewish congregation in Kiev, and a third person said he intended to organise similar prayer vigils at other synagogues in the country. It was a real moment of grace and blessing. As a result I appreciated, as never before, the significance of the all important role of the Jewish people who suffered so much during the holocaust.

A] PAUL'S ANGUISH OVER ISRAEL

There is a theory which some Christians espouse which is called replacement theology. It argues that the Christian Church has 'replaced' Israel (or the Jewish people) in God's plan of salvation as His chosen people. In its simplest expression, replacement theology could be articulated as follows: The Jews have rejected Christ; therefore God has rejected the Jews and the Church is now the 'New Israel.' Catholics reject this view because it is false and unscriptural. With its Vatican II declaration *Nostra Aetate* (In Our Time) par. 4 unequivocally professes, within a new theological

---

[20] Cf. James Mace Ward, *Priest, Politician, Collaborator: Jozef Tiso and the Making of Fascist Slovakia* (New York: Cornell University Press, 2013).

framework, the Jewish roots of Christianity. St John Paul II stated, 'The Jewish religion is not 'extrinsic' to us, but in a certain way is 'intrinsic' to our own religion. With Judaism therefore we have a relationship which we do not have with any other religion. You are our dearly beloved brothers and, in a certain way, it could be said that you are our elder brothers.'[21]

St Paul was Jewish to the core. As a passionate man, he had a fierce love for his people. It broke his heart when so many of his orthodox brothers and sisters not only failed to accept Jesus as their messiah, but were also strongly opposed to those Jews who had accepted Christ. It is profoundly moving to hear Paul, whose whole life centred on Christ, declare, 'I am speaking the truth in Christ - I am not lying; my conscience bears me witness in the Holy Spirit - that I have great sorrow and unceasing anguish in my heart. I could wish that I myself were accursed and cut off from Christ for the sake of my brothers, my kinsmen according to the flesh' (Rm 9:1-3). In other words he was willing to sacrifice what was most precious to him, namely his salvation in Christ, for the sake of his people. In Rm 11:1 Paul asked, 'Did God reject his people? By no means!' In Rm 11:11 he says, 'Again I ask: did they [the Jews] stumble so as to fall beyond recovery? Not at all!'

Par. 839 of the *Catechism of the Catholic Church*, confirms Paul's response in the following way,

> 'When she delves into her own mystery, the Church, the People of God in the New Covenant, discovers her link with the Jewish People, 'the first to hear the Word of God.' The Jewish faith, unlike other non-Christian religions, is already

---

[21] Discourse during visit to the Rome Synagogue, 13 April 1986

a response to God's revelation in the Old Covenant. To the
Jews 'belong the sonship, the glory, the covenants, the giving
of the law, the worship, and the promises; to them belong the
patriarchs, and of their race, according to the flesh, is the
Christ,' *for the gifts and the call of God are irrevocable* (my
italics).'

B] *Conversion of the Jews and the End Times*
Having examined the shortcomings of Israel, St. Paul answers the
question, 'Has God rejected his chosen people, the Israelites?' To
answer his question he went on to use an olive tree to illustrate his
point. Israelites were broken off for their unbelief (Rm 11:20), and
Gentiles were grafted in (Rm 11:17). Paul tells his Gentile readers
not to be arrogant toward the Jews (Rm 11:18, 20). Rather, they
should exercise humility (Rm 11:18), fear God (Rm 11:20), and
continue in kindness (Rm 11:22). The chapter is important and
requires a lot of commentary in order to arrive at a right understanding of its message. However fascinating it may be, some of
that exegesis is not really relevant as far as the subject matter of this
book is concerned.[22] The relevant verses come near the end of the
chapter. In Rm 11:25-26a St Paul wrote,

'Lest you be wise in your own sight, I do not want you to be
unaware of this mystery, brothers: a partial hardening has
come upon Israel, until the fullness of the Gentiles has come
in. And in this way all Israel will be saved.'

In his commentary on these verses Joseph A Fitzmyer points out
that there are two ways of understanding Paul's assertion that 'all

---

[22] For more on this see, Johannes Fichtenbauer, *The Mystery of the Olive Tree:*
Uniting Jews and Gentiles for Christ's Return (Luton: New Life Publishing , 2019).

Israel will be saved.' Firstly, it could imply that God will display an act of mercy to Israel independently of any acceptance of Jesus as Messiah or of a mass conversion to the Christian Gospel. Secondly, Paul may mean that the salvation of the Jews will come about as a result of grace through faith in Christ as the long awaited Messiah. Not surprisingly, Joseph Fitzmyer is of the opinion that the second of the two points is the only tenable one. Douglas J. Moo, who also has written a highly esteemed commentary on the epistle, calls Rm 11:26a 'the storm centre in the interpretation of Romans 9-11 and of the New Testament's teaching about the Jews and their future.' Moo interprets the passage as predicting a 'large-scale conversion of Jewish people at the end of this age' through 'faith in the gospel of Jesus their Messiah.' The clear implication is that this will happen when all the gentiles of the world have had an opportunity of responding to the gospel. As was noted earlier we are living at a paradoxical time when, in spite of the gentiles having had an opportunity of being evangelised, a great apostasy of people who have already been baptised is taking place. How long will it last? Paul indicates it will last until the mass conversion of the Jews. This is a very important point as far as this book is concerned. Paul is saying that before Jesus comes again, large numbers of Jews will freely accept him as their promised messiah. Speaking about this topic the *Catechism Of the Catholic Church* says in par. 674,

> 'The glorious Messiah's coming is suspended at every moment of history until his recognition by 'all Israel', for 'a hardening has come upon part of Israel' in their 'unbelief' toward Jesus . . . The 'full inclusion' of the Jews in the Messiah's salvation, in the wake of 'the full number of the Gentiles,' will enable the People of God to achieve 'the

measure of the stature of the fullness of Christ,' in which 'God may be all in all.'

Ever since the 1970s a growing number of Jewish people no longer stand at the door, because in the words of John Paul II they have crossed 'the threshold of faith' through 'total adherence to Jesus Christ.'[23] Surely it is one of the most significant and prophetic religious events of our time. Having heard the personal testimonies of a number of Messianic Jews I know that many of them had conversion experiences like that of St Paul on the road to Damascus. Without necessarily having been evangelised by a Christian, they had an encounter with Jesus, were persuaded that he was the Messiah, and accepted him as their saviour. I can say in this context that the Pontifical Commission for Religious Relations with the Jews issued the following statement, 'the Catholic Church neither conducts nor supports any specific institutional mission work directed towards Jews. While there is a principled rejection of an institutional Jewish mission, Christians are nonetheless called to bear witness to their faith in Jesus Christ also to Jews, although they should do so in a humble and sensitive manner, acknowledging that Jews are bearers of God's Word, and particularly in view of the great tragedy of the Shoah.'[24] In the meantime Cardinal Joseph Ratzinger said in a book entitled, *God and the World*, 'Israel still has a mission to accomplish today. We are in fact waiting for the moment when Israel, too, will say yes to Christ, but we also know

---

[23] John Paul II, par. 19 of The Apostolic Exhortation , *Catechesis in our Time.*

[24] Commission for Religious Relations with the Jews, par. 40 of *'The Gifts and the Calling of God Are Irrevocable,'* A reflection on Theological Questions pertaining to Catholic–Jewish relations on the occasion of the 50th anniversary of *Nostra Aetate* (no. 4).'

that while history still runs its course even this standing at the door fulfils a mission, one that is important for the world.'[25]

An entry entitled 'Messianic Judaism,' in *Wikipedia* contains a number of striking statistics. From 2003 to 2007, the movement grew from 150 Messianic places of worship in the United States to as many as 438, with over 100 in Israel and more worldwide. As of 2012, estimates of membership in the United States were between 175,000 and 250,000, between 10,000 and 20,000 members for Israel, and an estimated total worldwide membership of 350,000. Some of the Jews who are accepting Jesus as the Messiah are joining the Catholic Church, and refer to themselves as Hebrew Catholics. Roy Schoeman has published a book about some of them entitled *Honey From the Rock: Sixteen Jews find the Sweetness of Christ.*[26] Instead of talking about being converted to Catholicism, Schoeman describes himself as a fulfilled Jew who has found the fullness of his Jewish faith in the Catholic Church.

In 1998, a group of three Messianic Jewish leaders, together with Msgr. Peter Hocken, an English priest, and Johannes Fichtenbauer a Catholic deacon from Austria went to meet with Cardinal Josef Ratzinger in the Vatican. When the Messianic representatives shared their personal testimonies of how they had come to accept Jesus as their Messiah, the Cardinal listened carefully. In his book, *The Mystery of the Olive Tree*, Fichtenbauer says that Ratzinger responded,

'We theologians always knew that one day you (referring to the Messianic brothers) would need to appear. None of us

---

[25] (San Francisco: Ignatius Press, 2002), 149-50.

[26] (San Francisco: Ignatius Press, 2007).

could imagine how this would happen.' He mentioned that as he was listening to their witness, an important question had to be raised: is this Messianic witness an authentic experience? If this phenomenon is proved authentic, does that mean that this Movement is an eschatological sign? All present in the room were astounded! Who could expect such words – especially when one considers who was speaking. In essence, what the Cardinal was indirectly saying was that even though the Holy Spirit throughout the centuries has preserved the Church, the Church today, because she lacks her Jewish component, is still incomplete.'[27]

Since then the Church has not only come to the conclusion that the Messianic experience is genuine, it also believes that it is a likely intimation of the coming of the end times.

Christians need to pray for the Jews. Hebrew Catholic St Edith Stein was an archetypal example during World War II. When she learned what the Nazis were doing to her people she prayed fervently for them. She knew that they were related by blood to Jesus if not by faith. As a woman who shared the same blood (cf. Eph 5:29), but who also believed in Jesus as the Messiah, she recognised that her brothers and sisters were going to endure an unjust and diabolical baptism of suffering and death. Edith wrote: 'I spoke to our Saviour and told Him that I knew that it was His Cross that was now being laid on the Jewish people. Most did not understand it, but those who did understand must accept it willingly in the name of all. I wanted to do that, let Him only show me how. When the service was over I had an interior conviction that I had been heard. But in what the bearing of the Cross was to consist I did not yet know. I

[27] (Luton: New Life Publishing, 2019), 92.

was almost relieved to find myself now involved in the common fate of my people.'[28] Because of the growing anti-Jewish strictures in Germany in 1939, Stein was smuggled across the border to the Netherlands to the Carmelite Convent in Echt. There she wrote her last will on June 9, 1939: 'Even now I accept the death that God has prepared for me in complete submission and with joy as being his most holy will for me. *I ask the Lord to accept my life and my death so that the Lord will be accepted by his people and his kingdom may come in glory.*' In 1942, like so many of her fellow Jews, Edith was murdered in Auschwitz Concentration Camp. Surely, her sacrifice as a representative of her people, acted as a down payment on behalf of her fellow Jews and as a graced go-between who providentially prepared the way for all the Jewish conversions that have taken place in recent years. As Paul said in Rm 11:33, 'For God has consigned all to disobedience, that he may have mercy on all' and again in Rm 5:20, 'Where sin abounds, grace abounds much more.' Jewish conversions to Christ are not only an expression of the unmerited mercy of God, they also have great eschatological significance.

RESURRECTION OF THE DEAD[29]

The doctrine of the resurrection of the dead is an essential aspect of Paul's eschatology. He believed that since 'flesh and blood cannot inherit the kingdom of God,' believers must have their bodies 'changed' when Christ returns to usher them into God's eternal kingdom (1 Cor 15:50-52), while believers who are living

---

[28] Posselt, Teresia Renata de Spiritu Sancto, OCD. *Edith Stein* (Washington, DC: Institute of Carmelite Studies, 2005) 116.

[29] For a brief summary of Biblical thought on the subject see, Timothy S Johnson, 'Death and Resurrection,' in *New International Version Zondervan Study Bible* (Grand Rapids: Zondervan, 2015), 2670-2671.

will have their bodies raised and transformed and taken up to meet the Lord in the air (1 Thess 4:17) while believers who have died will have their bodies raised and transformed (1 Cor15:52; 1 Thess 4:16). N. T. Wright stresses in his book, *Surprised by Hope*, that Paul did not believe in a Platonic or Gnostic manner in a spiritual, non-material body. He says that, 'it can be demonstrated in great detail, philologically and exegetically, that this is precisely not what Paul meant. The contrast he makes is not between what we could mean by a present physical body and what we would mean by a future spiritual one, but between a present body animated by the normal human soul and a future body animated by God's Spirit.'[30] Scripture asserts that resurrection will not be confined to believers, all humans will participate in it (Jn 5:28-30; Rev 20:5-6). Believers will be raised 'imperishable' (1 Cor15:52), destined for eternal fellowship with God in the new Jerusalem. The unbelieving dead will be consigned to hell '*gehenna*' where they will experience unending alienation and frustration.

Conclusion

We can draw this chapter to a close by adverting to the revised prayer for the Jewish people which is said in Catholic churches on Good Friday. 'Let us pray also for the Jewish people, to whom the Lord our God spoke first, that he may grant them to advance in love of his name and in faithfulness to his covenant. Almighty and ever-living God, who bestowed your promises on Abraham and his descendants, hear graciously the prayers of your Church, that the people you first made your own may attain the fullness of redemption. Through Christ our Lord. Amen.'

---

[30] (New York: Harper/Collins, 2008),44.

FIVE

THE APOCALYPTIC OF
STS JOHN AND PETER

T HE BOOK OF REVELATION IS THE LAST ONE IN THE BIBLE, though not the last to be written. That distinction belongs to the second letter of Peter. Arguably Revelation is the most apocalyptic book of a prophetic kind in the entire Bible. It is also the most Jewish with at least 800 references to the Old Testament. Some of the fathers of the Church believed that the Book of Revelation was written by the author of the fourth Gospel. This identification, however, was denied by other Fathers. It is possible and even probable that it was written by a disciple of John on the island of Patmos in Greece. Scholars have also been long divided about the date of the book's composition. Early Christian tradition favoured 90 AD during the time of the emperor Domitian. Others opted for an earlier date of about 60 AD, and therefore, before the destruction of the temple and the city of Jerusalem.

Origen (184–253 AD) said, 'Who can read the revelation granted to John without being amazed at the hidden depth of the ineffable mysteries, a depth apparent even to the person who does not understand what the text says?'[1] That said, it has to be admitted that the Book of Revelation is a notoriously difficult one to interpret. G. K. Chesterton wrote, 'Though St. John the Evangelist saw many strange monsters in his vision, he saw no creature so

---

[1] *On First Principles,* 4.2.4.

wild as one of his own commentators.'[2] Speaking about non-fundamentalist scripture interpretation the *Catechism of the Catholic Church* says in pars 109-10, 'In Sacred Scripture, God speaks to man in a human way. To interpret Scripture correctly, the reader must be attentive to what the human authors truly wanted to affirm, and to what God wanted to reveal to us by their words. In order to discover *the sacred authors' intention*, the reader must take into account the conditions of their time and culture, the literary genres in use at that time, and the modes of feeling, speaking and narrating then current. For the fact is that truth is differently presented and expressed in the various types of historical writing, in prophetical and poetical texts, and in other forms of literary expression.'

The term apocalyptic is derived from a Greek word meaning 'revelatory.' It can be argued that there are four ways in which the *Book of Revelation* can be interpreted. They have been succinctly summarised by Archbishop Averky Tuschev (1906-1976) of the Russian Orthodox Church. The words in brackets are technical theological terms that are used to describe different approaches to interpretation. The Archbishop wrote that one may divide all commentaries on Revelation into four groups.

1. Some of them refer all the visions and symbols of the Apocalypse to the 'last times' – the end of the world, the appearance of the Antichrist, and the Second Coming of Christ. (Futurist)

2. Others give the Apocalypse a purely historical significance, referring all the visions to the historical events of the first

---

[2] *Orthodoxy* (New York: Doubleday, 1908), 17.

century – to the times of the persecutions raised against the Church by the pagan emperors. (Preterist)

3. A third group strives to find the realisation of apocalyptic prophecies in the historical events of recent times. In their opinion, for example, the Pope of Rome is Antichrist, and all the apocalyptic misfortunes are announced in particular for the Church of Rome, etc. (Historicist)

4. A fourth group, finally, sees in the Apocalypse only an allegory, considering that the visions described in it have not so much prophetic as moral meaning, and allegory is introduced only to increase the impression, with the aim of striking the imagination of readers. (Idealist)

The most comprehensive interpretation of apocalyptic texts is likely to be one that unites what is valid in all these approaches, keeping in mind that, as the ancient commentators and Fathers of the Church clearly taught that, taken together, the content of the Apocalypse is directed to the last part of the history of the world.[3] The Book of Revelation contains many valuable teachings which challenge its readers to repent of and to resist compromise with the secular world; spiritual complacency; and false teaching. It encourages believers to hold fast to their witness to Jesus, to steadfastly endure trials, and to firmly hope in God's future reign (Rev 1:9; 2:10; 3:11; 12:17; 14:12; 22:7). While all of this is interesting we will confine ourselves to some of the main things the author had to say about the end times.

A THOUSAND YEARS OF PEACE

Arguably, the first six verses of the twentieth chapter of Revelation,

---

[3] *The Apocalypse: In the Teachings of Ancient Christianity* (Platina, CA: St Herman Pr, 1996), 53-54.

are the most important as far as the subject matter of this book is concerned. They read,

> 'Then I saw an angel coming down from heaven, holding in his hand the key to the bottomless pit and a great chain. And he seized the dragon, that ancient serpent, who is the devil and Satan, and bound him for a thousand years, and threw him into the pit, and shut it and sealed it over him, so that he might not deceive the nations any longer, until the thousand years were ended. After that he must be released for a little while. Then I saw thrones, and seated on them were those to whom the authority to judge was committed. Also I saw the souls of those who had been beheaded for the testimony of Jesus and for the word of God, and who had not worshiped the beast or its image and had not received its mark on their foreheads or their hands. They came to life and reigned with Christ for a thousand years. The rest of the dead did not come to life until the thousand years were ended. This is the first resurrection. Blessed and holy is the one who shares in the first resurrection! Over such the second death has no power, but they will be priests of God and of Christ, and they will reign with him for a thousand years.'

The 'millenium' is the thousand years mentioned in Rev 20:1-6. The word is a combination of two Latin words *mille* (thousand) and *annum* (years). From the earliest times Christian interpreters have been divided over their understanding of the nature and timing of the millennium relative to the second coming of Jesus. There are three main views.

- In premillennialism Jesus returns before his thousand year reign on earth. In 1944, the Catholic Church condemned even a mitigated form of pre millenarianism (DBS 3839)'[4]

- In postmillennialism, Jesus returns after an earthly golden age.

- In amillennialism, the millennium is a symbolic time between the ascension of Jesus and his return, when deceased believers reign with Christ in heaven. The term amillennialism literally means 'no millennium,' since the prefix 'a' in Greek negates the term that it precedes.

Amillennialism, which owes a lot to the theology of St Augustine, is espoused by Catholic, Orthodox and many mainline Protestant Christians. This understanding regards the thousand year period as a figurative duration for Christ's reign. There will be no literal historical reign of Christ on earth for 1000 years. The spiritual reign of Christ and His saints is already in existence for the period of time between Christ's two advents. The kingdom of God is in the here and now, present in and through the Church. Amillennialism teaches that the binding of Satan, described in Revelation, has already occurred and he has been prevented by the spread of the gospel from 'deceiving the nations' by the spread of the gospel. According to the amillennial interpretation of the Parable of the Wheat and Tares, good and evil will coexist in every historical era and even in the church. Commenting on this notion, scripture scholar Ray Brown wrote in his *An Introduction to the New Testament*, 'The larger, established churches remain convinced that, although the final stage in the divine plan will be accomplished through Jesus Christ, the thousand years are symbolic and no one knows

---

[4] *An Introduction to the New Testament* (New York: Doubleday, 1996), 802.

when or how the end of the world will come. Acts 1:7 sets the tone: 'It is not for you to know times and seasons that have been set by the Father's own authority.'[5]

THE RAPTURE: A MISGUIDED THEOLOGICAL THEORY

It is worth mentioning that some Protestant evangelicals espouse a premillennial interpretation of Rev 20:1-6 which is sometimes referred to as dispensationalism. This theory was developed by John Nelson Darby (1800-1882). He was originally ordained a priest in the Church of Ireland, and later became a co-founder of the Plymouth Brethren. He came to believe that all of time can be divided into seven distinguishable dispensations namely, Paradise, Noah, Abraham, Israel, Gentiles, the Spirit, and the Millennium. We are waiting for the outworking of the final dispensation. Darby also believed that there were two totally distinct divine plans for history, in the scriptures, one concerning an earthly people, i.e., Israel, the other a heavenly people, i.e., the Church. God's plan for Israel was revealed through a series of covenants with people such as Adam, Moses and David which pointed to the establishment of a Messianic kingdom on earth. But when the Messiah came in the person of Jesus, most of Israel rejected him. Darby maintained that God then postponed the kingdom, turned away from Israel and created out of the Gentiles a new people, the Church. According to this postponement theory, God will only resume his dealings with Israel when the building of the Church is completed and the saved have been raptured, i.e., raised into heaven. Then the events of the last days will kick in: namely the great tribulation, the rise of Antichrist, the battle of Armageddon, and then the Second Coming

---

[5] (New York: Doubleday, 1997), 802.

of Christ who will bind Satan and the set up the millennial kingdom.[6]

These mistaken beliefs to do with two comings of Christ before and after the great tribulation have influenced many evangelical Protestants in the United States. In the twentieth and twenty first centuries premillennial dispensationalism has spawned a series of sixteen *Left Behind* books which were co-authored by Tim LaHaye and Jerry B. Jenkins. Seven of the books in the adult series have reached number one on the bestseller lists of the *New York Times*. Four movies have been based on the rapture theory, one of which is called *Left Behind*. It was released in 2014. It would be amusing if it were not so sadly misleading from a doctrinal point of view. For instance, in one scene in the movie Rayford Steele, a pilot, is seen on one of his flights during which strange things happen. Several people, including his co-pilot Chris Smith, Kimmy, one of the flight attendants, and all the children on board, simply disappear, leaving their clothing and personal effects behind. The remaining passengers panic and demand answers. Steele does his best to reassure the passengers that he will pass on information as soon as he has any. However, he has difficulty establishing radio contact with anyone on the ground, until eventually he is told that it is due to the fact that many people have disappeared all over the world.

Catholics like many Orthodox and Protestant Christians do not subscribe to a belief in a pre-tribulation rapture.[7] This theological

---

6 See *Dictionary of Christianity in America*, edited by Daniel G. Reid, Robert D. Linder, Bruce L. Shelley and Harry S. Stout (InterVarsity Press, 1990).

[7] This evangelical view is critiqued in T. L Frazier's *A Second Look at the Second Coming: Sorting Through the Speculations* (Ben Lomond CA: Conciliar Press, 1999).

theory is based on an incorrect interpretation of a number of texts, notably Mt 24:40-41; 1 Thess 4:16-17; Rev 3:10. As well known Protestant scripture scholar, Ben Witherington III has pointed out, there is no substantial support for the notion of a rapture in scripture. Speaking about the fundamentalist approach of the dispensationalists he wryly observed, 'a text without a context is a pretext for having it mean whatever you want it to mean.'[8] While Catholics and many other Christians reject the notion of the rapture, of course they do believe that at the end of time the living and the dead will be raised either to be with Christ or to be forever separated from him. For a good critique of rapture theology, from an Orthodox Christian point of view, see T. L. Frazier's *A Second Look at the Second Coming: Sorting Through the Speculations.*[9]

GOG, MAGOG AND ARMAGEDDON
In Rev 20:7-9 we read,

> 'And when the thousand years are ended, Satan will be released from his prison and will come out to deceive the nations that are at the four corners of the earth, Gog and Magog, to gather them for battle; their number is like the sand of the sea. And they marched up over the broad plain of the earth and surrounded the camp of the saints and the beloved city, but fire came down from heaven and consumed them, and the devil who had deceived them was thrown into the lake of fire and sulphur where the beast and the false prophet were, and they will be tormented day and night forever and ever.'

[8] Ben Witherington III , 'Where Did Rapture Theology Come From?' *YouTube*, *https://www.youtube.com/watch?v=d_cVXdr8mVs* (Accessed 14/2/2019).

[9] (Ben Lomond CA: Conciliar Press, 1999).

Clearly, mention of Gog and Magog in this text is a reference back to Ezek 38 which we examined in chapter two. Whether the precise historical application of Ezekiel's prophecy can be identified with the Romans and their emperor as was the case in early Christian writings, such as those of Eusebius, is debatable. When the Roman Empire became Christian, Ambrose (d.397) identified Gog with the Goths, and Jerome (d. 420) identified Gog with the Scythians. Who Gog and Magog were supposed to be is not all that important. The point is this, a vicious, diabolical enemy, seemingly an overwhelming evil power, would come against the Lord's people. But Israel would not be vanquished. God would intervene and be their Saviour. So, in like fashion God will suddenly and victoriously intervene in the end times when evil will seem to be in the ascendency.

In this context it makes sense to advert to what Revelation says about a place called Megiddo. It is known for its historical, geographical, and theological importance, especially under its Greek name Armageddon. I can recall that on the memorable day when I visited the top of Mt Tabor which rises 1,843 ft above sea level, I could see Megiddo in the distance. Because of its geographical position it has been the site of many battles, e.g., British General Allenby won an allied victory there in 1918, and he was known afterwards as Allenby of Armageddon. The one New Testament reference to Armageddon is to be found in Revelation 16:14-15 where it says, 'These are demonic spirits, performing signs, who go abroad to the kings of the whole world, to assemble them for battle on the great day of God the Almighty.' It is interesting to note that the evil spirits mentioned are associated with performing signs in much the same way as the Antichrist that Jesus spoke about in Mt 24:24, and Paul spoke about in 2 Thess

2:9-10. The verse makes no specific mention of any armies which will one day gather in this place, but instead seems to predict only that kings will meet there. However in view of the fact that Rev 16:14, tells us, 'they go out to the kings of the whole world, to gather them for the battle on the great day of God Almighty' we have reason to believe that some sort of apocalyptic battle will take place. Read in a literal way, these verses seem to imply that a great military struggle between the forces of good and evil will take place on the plains of Megiddo. When understood in a literal rather than a symbolical way, these verses have given rise to a lot of far fetched speculation in some Protestant fundamentalist circles. As we saw in 2 Thess 2:8 Paul said of the lawless one that, 'the Lord Jesus will overthrow [him] with the breath of his mouth.'

THE FINAL TRIBULATION

In Rev 7:14 there is a reference to the redeemed in heaven as 'they who have come out of the great tribulation.' That verse alludes to Dan 12:1 which says, 'And there shall be a time of trouble, such as never has been since there was a nation till that time' and to Mt 24:31, 'For then there will be great tribulation, such as has not been from the beginning of the world until now, no, and never will be.' At this point it is worth recalling a point that was made earlier in the book about the paradoxical fact that the end time, is present in an anticipatory way in the form of minor tribulations of one kind or another until the appointed time of the great tribulation that will precede the second coming of Jesus.

A] MINOR TRIBULATIONS

Anyone familiar with Church history will know that the Church has endured many times of tribulation in the past. For example I saw a very interesting movie entitled, *The Day of the Siege: September*

Eleven 1683 which highlighted the prophetic leadership of a Capuchin priest, Bl. Marco d'Aviano (1631-1699) during the Ottoman attack on Vienna in 1683. Sultan Mehmet IV wrote to Fr. D'Aviano at the time, 'We order you to wait for us in your Viennese residence so that We can decapitate you...We will exterminate You and all Your followers... Children and adults will be equally exposed to the most atrocious tortures before being finished off in the most ignominious way imaginable...'. In the event the forces of the Holy League, under Poland's King Jan Sobieski, roundly defeated the 300,000 Mohammedan invaders at the Battle of Vienna. Afterwards Sobieski summed up his victory in these words: 'I came, I saw, God conquered!'

In Oct 2016 I realised a life time ambition when I had an opportunity to visit the Holy Land. One of my more notable memories had to do with a visit to Mount Tabor. While there I recalled the words which God the Father addressed to us all through the apostles Peter, James and John when Jesus was transfigured by light before them. He said, 'This is my Son, whom I love; with him I am well pleased. *Listen to him!*' (Mt 17:5). I think I am right in saying that the words 'Listen to him' are the only words that the Father ever addressed directly to human kind, Having recalled those words I went into the Catholic church on the top of the mountain, sat near the back and said, 'Lord Jesus, God the Father told me to listen to you, so I do not want to leave this church until you speak to me.' Shortly, afterwards I received a memorable message from the Lord. It said, 'Though your sufferings may be long and hard to bear, they are only like a pin prick compared to the tidal wave of joy which will envelop you. In those days you will have no recollection of your suffering,' As soon as I heard those words inwardly, I wondered were they addressed in a specific way to me. Then I seemed to understand, that no, they were addressed to people in a more general way and were about a time of great tribulation to come in the world, followed ultimately if not immediately by doomsday, and then by 'a new heavens and a new earth' (Rev 21:1).

Almost immediately, I recalled a scripture text in which Jesus said, 'When a woman is giving birth, she has sorrow because her hour has come, but when she has delivered the baby, she no longer remembers the anguish, for joy that a human being has been born into the world' (Jn 16:21-22). Since then, four similar texts have come to mind. In the first St Paul says, 'I consider that the sufferings of this present time are not worth comparing with the glory that is to be revealed to us' (Rm 8:18) and in the second he says, 'Our light and momentary troubles are achieving for us an eternal glory that far outweighs them all' (2 Cor 4:17). Thirdly, 1 Pt 5:10 says, 'And after you have suffered a little while, the God of all grace, who has called you to his eternal glory in Christ, will himself restore, confirm, strengthen, and establish you.' Finally, Jesus described the turbulent events that will occur near the end of the world in Mt 24:8 where he said, 'All these are but the beginning of the birth pains.'

As a result of that experience in Israel I indicated in *Prophecy: Truth for Today, Light for Tomorrow,* how, like a number of others, I believe that the world is due to experience yet another cleansing and purifying time of tribulation in the relatively near future. I was interested to see that Desmond A. Birch says in the lengthy introduction to his book *Trial, Tribulation & Triumph Before, During and after the Antichrist,* 'The prophesied impending signs of this *Minor* yet worldwide Chastisement do *appear* to be growing. Unlike the prophesied signs of the Major Chastisement of Antichrist, all the signs of a minor tribulation do *appear* to be *partially* in place.'[10] I was also interested to see that in the course of a general audience on Sept. 10, 2003, St. John Paul II said, 'After purification through trial and suffering, the dawn of a new era is about to break.' John Paul thought that it would be made possible by the new evangelisation which would bring about 'a civilisation of love,' and a 'new Springtime for Christianity.' It will be a time when Christianity will blossom again in unity and peace following a time of adversity.

B] THE GREAT TRIBULATION

The times of tribulation that afflict the church and the world on a regular basis are dress rehearsals for the great tribulation which will occur just before the end of the world as we know it. In the earlier chapter on St Paul we saw how a great apostasy is going to take place before the end. Believers, will be subject to persecution and will be tempted to embrace the false teachings and values of the Antichrist. Writing about this Adso Abbot of Montier-en-Der (c. 915-992) wrote,

'He will arouse universal persecution against the Christians and all the elect. He will lift himself up against the faithful in three ways, that is, by terror, by gifts, and by prodigies. To those who believe in him he will give much gold and silver. Those he is not able to corrupt with gifts, he will overcome with terror; those he cannot overcome with terror, he will try to seduce with signs and prodigies. Those he cannot seduce with prodigies, he will cruelly torture and miserably put to death in the sight of all. 'Then there will be tribulation such

---

[10] (Goleta CA: Queenship Publishing, 1996), lxiv.

as has not been on earth from when the nations began to exist up to that time. Then those who are in the field will flee to the mountains, and he who is on the roof will not go down into his house to take anything from it.' Then every faithful Christian who will be discovered will either deny God, or, if he will remain faithful, will perish, whether through sword, or fiery furnace, or serpents, or beasts, or through some other kind of torture. This terrible and fearful tribulation will last for three and a half years in the whole world. 'Then the days will be shortened for the sake of the elect, for unless the Lord had shortened those days, mankind would not have been saved.'[11]

Speaking about the Church's ultimate trial pars 675-677 of the *Catechism of the Catholic Church* says,

'Before Christ's second coming the Church must pass through a final trial that will shake the faith of many believers. The persecution that accompanies her pilgrimage on earth will unveil the 'mystery of iniquity' in the form of a religious deception offering men an apparent solution to their problems at the price of apostasy from the truth. . . . The Church will enter the glory of the kingdom only through this final Passover, when she will follow her Lord in his death and Resurrection. The kingdom will be fulfilled, then, not by a historic triumph of the Church through a progressive ascendancy, but only by God's victory over the final unleashing of evil, which will cause his Bride to come down from heaven. God's triumph over the revolt of evil will take

---

[11] See Bernard McGinn, 'Adso's biography of Antichrist,' in *Antichrist: Two Thousand Years of the Human Fascination with Evil* (San Francisco: Harper Collins, 1994), 100-103.

the form of the Last Judgment after the final cosmic upheaval of this passing world.'

In previous chapters we noted the fact that the catastrophic events which will be characteristic of the final persecution will take the form of unprecedented earthquakes, wars, famines, cosmic disturbances etc,

ST PETER ON THE END TIMES

There are a number of graphic apocalyptic descriptions of the end of history in the scriptures. It is hard to know whether they are merely symbolic descriptions of spiritual things or prophetic anticipations of actual events that are yet to take place, e.g., as a result of nuclear war or a large comet colliding with earth. Among those descriptions is the following one from 2 Peter 3:7-13,

> 'The present heavens and earth are reserved for fire, being kept for the day of judgment and destruction of ungodly men. . . Since everything will be destroyed in this way, what kind of people ought you to be? You ought to live holy and godly lives as you look forward to the day of God and speed its coming. That day will bring about the destruction of the heavens by fire, and the elements will melt in the heat. But in keeping with his promise we are looking forward to a new heaven and a new earth, the home of righteousness.'

Peter's mention of fire is an image of God's judgement which was mentioned in Is 30:30; 66:15-16; Nah 1:6; Zeph 1:18, 3:8. The notion of the world being destroyed by fire is not fanciful. From a scientific point of view it could take two forms. Firstly, if a worldwide nuclear war broke out. Besides the immediate destruction of cities by nuclear blasts, the potential aftermath of nuclear explosions could involve firestorms, a long lasting winter, widespread radiation sickness from fallout, and the temporary loss of much modern technology due to electromagnetic pulses. Secondly, a large asteroid from space could strike the earth. We know that this happened 66 million years ago, possibly in the Gulf of Mexico's Yucatán Peninsula. The impact of the nine mile wide object wiped out some three-quarters of the plant and animal species on Earth, including the dinosaurs. In April 2018, the B 612 Foundation in California reported 'It's 100 per cent certain we'll be hit by an asteroid, but we're not 100% certain when.' In the same year, astrophysicist Stephen Hawking, said in his final book *Brief Answers to the Big Questions*, that an asteroid collision is the biggest threat to the planet. It has been estimated that if an asteroid with a diameter of 500 km. crashed into the Pacific Ocean, the impact would dislocate 10 km of the earth's crust. The shockwave would travel at hypersonic speeds. Debris would be blasted into low Earth orbit, and return to destroy the surface of the Earth. A firestorm would engulf Earth, thereby vaporising all life in its way.' In the past the planet was virtually destroyed by water during the flood at the time of Noah. St Peter tells us that at the end of the world it will be destroyed by fire.

CONCLUSION

The value of the Book of Revelation is especially relevant when our faith and our Church seem to be ever more marginalised in our present day secularised society. If indeed these are the final days before Christ's return, then we can expect to be increasingly marginalised in an increasingly godless world. In days such as these, however, the inspired author of Revelation reassures us that

Christ and his Church will overcome Satan and his demonic forces in a definitive way. Knowing this to be true, T. L. Frazier counsels, 'even, though our prayers *seem* to bounce off the closed doors of heaven, though God's saints *seem* to be defeated, though evil *seems* to conquer everywhere we look, the reality is just the opposite. Our prayers are coming to the very throne of God (Rev 6:10); we are reigning even now on earth (Rev 5:10) as well as in heaven (Rev 20:4); and we learn that ultimately it is evil itself that will be conquered and thrown into the lake of fire.'[12]

[12] *A Second Look at the Second Coming* (Ben Lomond, CA: Conciliar Press, 1999), 325.

SIX

SOME RECENT CHURCH LEADERS ON THE END-TIMES

I T MAY COME AS A SURPRISE TO MANY READERS to find how a number of relatively recent leaders in the Catholic and Anglican Church have suggested that the second coming of Jesus may be close at hand. In this chapter we will look at what a number of them have said while commenting briefly on their views..

1] St Pius X

In his 1903 Encyclical *E Supremi* (On the Restoration of All things in Christ), Pope St Pius X wrote in par 5,

> 'When all this is considered there is good reason to fear lest this great perversity may be as it were a foretaste, and perhaps the beginning of those evils which are reserved for the last days; and that there may be already in the world the 'Son of Perdition' of whom the Apostle speaks (2 Thess. 2:3). Such, in truth, is the audacity and the wrath employed everywhere in persecuting religion, in combating the dogmas of the faith, in a brazen effort to uproot and destroy all relations between man and the Divinity! While, on the other hand, and this according to the same apostle is the distinguishing mark of Antichrist, man has with infinite temerity put himself in the place of God, raising himself above all that is called God; in such a manner that although he cannot utterly extinguish

in himself all knowledge of God, he has treated God's majesty with contempt and, as it were, made of the universe a temple wherein he himself is to be adored. 'He sits in the temple of God, showing himself as if he were God (2 Thess. 2:2).'

Arguably, what evoked those comments was the Pope's belief that Modernism[1] posed a great threat to the Church which Pius considered the 'synthesis of all heresies.' It is quite clear that he was deeply troubled by modern forms of humanistic messianism. St Pius also said,

'I saw one of my successors taking to flight over the bodies of his brethren. He will take refuge in disguise somewhere; and after a short retirement he will die a cruel death. The present wickedness of the world is only the beginning of the sorrows which must take place before the end of the world.'[2]

Implicit in that prophecy is the suggestion that the Vatican will be attacked at some time in the future and that the Pope will be killed. That will be a sign that the end times are about to kick in. Although he died in 1914, Pope Pius probably had intimations of the devastating Word War that was about to break out in Europe.

2] St John Henry Newman

We noted in chapter four how in his Advent Sermons on Antichrist, which were published in a book entitled *Discussions and Arguments*

---

[1] Modernism was a movement in the final years of the 19th century and first decade of the 20th that sought to reinterpret traditional Catholic teaching in the light of 19th-century philosophical, historical, and psychological theories and called for freedom of conscience.

[2] Yves Dupont, *Catholic Prophecy: The Coming Chastisement* (Rockford; Tan, 2009), 22.

in 1872, St Henry Newman quoted from a very interesting letter written by Anglican Bishop Horsley. It was about the subject of an impending apostasy in the Christian Church.

It strikes me that what Bishop Horsley said found an echo over a hundred years later in prophetic words spoken by Joseph Ratzinger (Benedict XVI) in the course of a broadcast on German radio in 1969. While he was still an Anglican Newman wrote,

> 'Surely, there is at this day a confederacy of evil, marshalling its hosts from all parts of the world, organising itself, taking its measures, enclosing the Church of Christ as in a net, and preparing the way for a general Apostasy from it. Whether this very Apostasy is to give birth to Antichrist, or whether he is still to be delayed, as he has already been delayed so long, we cannot know; but at any rate this Apostasy, and all its tokens and instruments, are of the Evil One, and savour of death. Far be it from any of us to be of those simple ones who are taken in that snare which is circling around us! Far be it from us to be seduced with the fair promises in which Satan is sure to hide his poison! Do you think he is so unskilful in his craft, as to ask you openly and plainly to join him in his warfare against the Truth? No; he offers you baits to tempt you. He promises you civil liberty; he promises you equality; he promises you trade and wealth; he promises you a remission of taxes; he promises you reform. This is the way in which he conceals from you the kind of work to which he is putting you; he tempts you to rail against your rulers and superiors; he does so himself, and induces you to imitate him; or he promises you illumination, he offers you knowledge, science, philosophy, enlargement of mind. He scoffs at times

gone by; he scoffs at every institution which reveres them. He prompts you what to say, and then listens to you, and praises you, and encourages you. He bids you mount aloft. He shows you how to become as gods. Then he laughs and jokes with you, and gets intimate with you; he takes your hand, and gets his fingers between yours, and grasps them, and then you are his.'[3]

Those who live in eager expectation of Christ's coming at the time of their personal death and later in the second coming hear the daily call to be converted from the ways of the world to the ways of God. As it says at the foot of the Papal Cross in the Phoenix Park in Dublin, 'be converted every day.'

2] Pius XII
Cardinal Eugene Pacelli (Pope Pius XII) is reported to have said in 1931,

'I am worried by the Blessed Virgin's messages to Lucy of Fatima. This persistence of Mary about the dangers which menace the Church is a Divine warning against the suicide of altering the Faith . . . A day will come when the civilised world will deny its God, when the Church will doubt as Peter doubted. She will be tempted to believe that man has become God. In our churches, Christians will search in vain for the red lamp where God awaits them, like Mary Magdalene weeping before the empty tomb, they will ask, 'Where have they taken Him?'[4]

---

[3] 'The Patristical Idea of Antichrist in Four Lectures,' in *Discussions and Arguments on Various Subjects* (London: Pickering, 1872).

[4] Georges Roche & Phillipe Saint Germaine, *Pie XII Devant L'Histoire* (Paris: Robert Lafont, 1972), 52-53.

When Pacelli became Pope Pius XII he said in an encyclical which was promulgated in 1951,

> 'You are well aware that almost the whole human race is today allowing itself to be driven into two opposing camps, for Christ or against Christ. The human race is involved today in a supreme crisis, which will issue in its salvation by Christ, or in its dire destruction. The preachers of the Gospel are using their talents and energy to extend the Kingdom of Christ; but there are other preachers who, since they profess materialism and reject all hope of eternal happiness, are trying to drag men down to an abject condition.'[5]

In his 1957 Easter Message Pope Pius XII said,

> 'There are numerous signs that Your return is not far off.'

As we note below St John Paul II said something very similar in 1976.[6]

3] ARCHBISHOP FULTON SHEEHAN

When I was a boy I was aware that Bishop Fulton Sheehan was a charismatic teacher of the Catholic faith. However, in adult life I was surprised that this saintly man had prophetic gifts. For example, on Jan 26th 1947 Archbishop Fulton Sheehan preached a remarkable sermon entitled, 'The Signs of the Times.' At one point he spoke in a prophetic way about the Antichrist. This extended quotation illustrates the point,

> 'Our Lord tells us that He will be so much like Himself, that

---

[5] *Evangelii Paecones* (1951) par. 70.

[6] Ralph Martin, *The Final Confrontation* (London: St Paul Distribution UK, 2016).

he would deceive even the elect-and certainly no devil we have ever seen in picture books could deceive even the elect. How will he come in this new age to win followers to his religion? He will come disguised as the Great Humanitarian; he will talk peace, prosperity and plenty not as means to lead us to God, but as ends in themselves He will write books on the new idea of God to suit the way people live; induce faith in astrology so as to make not the will but the stars responsible for sins; he will explain Guilt away psychologically as inhibited eroticism, make men shrink in shame if their fellowmen say they are not broadminded and liberal; he will be so broadminded as to identify tolerance with indifference to right and wrong, truth and error; he will spread the lie that men will never be better until they make society better and thus have selfishness to provide fuel for the next revolution; he will foster science but only to have armament makers use one marvel of science to destroy another; he will foster more divorces under the disguise that another partner is 'vital;' he will increase love for love and decrease love for person; he will invoke religion to destroy religion; he will even speak of Christ and say that he was the greatest man who ever lived; his mission he will say will be to liberate men from the servitudes of superstition and Fascism: which he will never define; he will organise children's games, tell people who they should and should not marry and un-marry, who should bear children and who should not; he will benevolently draw chocolate bars from his pockets for the little ones and bottles of milk for the Hottentots (i.e. people of Western Cape Colony in South Africa); he will tempt Christians with the same three temptations which he tempted Christ: The temptation to turn

stones into bread as an earthly Messiah will become the
temptation to sell freedom for security, as bread became a
political weapon, and only those who think his way may eat;
the temptation to work a miracle by recklessly throwing
Himself from a steeple will become a plea to desert the lofty
pinnacles of truth where faith and reason reign, for those
lower depths where the masses live on slogans and propaganda. He wants no proclamation of immutable principles
from the lofty heights of a Church, but mass organisation
through propaganda where only a common man directs
the idiosyncrasies of common men. Opinions not truths,
commentators not teachers, Gallup polls not principles,
nature not grace - and to these golden calves will men toss
themselves from their Christ.'

The following year 1948 the Archbishop wrote in like manner,

'We are living in the days of the Apocalypse, the last days of
our era. The two great forces, the Mystical Body of Christ and
the Mystical Body of the anti-Christ are beginning to draw
battle lines for the catastrophic contest.'[7] '[Satan] will set up
a counter-church which will be the ape of the [Catholic]
Church ... It will have all the notes and characteristics of the
Church, but in reverse and emptied of its divine content.

The False prophet will have a religion without a cross. A
religion without a world to come. A religion to destroy
religions. There will be a counterfeit Church. Christ's Church
the Catholic Church will be one; and the false Prophet will

[7] Flynn T & L. *The Thunder of Justice* (Sterling, VA : Maxkol Communications,
1993), 20.

create the other. The False Church will be worldly, ecumenical, and global. It will be a loose federation of churches and religions, forming some type of global association. A world parliament of Churches. It will be emptied of all Divine content, it will be the mystical body of the anti-Christ. The Mystical Body on earth today will have its Judas Iscariot, and he will be the false prophet. Satan will recruit him from our Bishops.

The Antichrist will not be so called; otherwise he would have no followers. He will not wear red tights, nor vomit sulphur, nor carry a trident nor wave an arrowed tail as Mephistopheles in Faust. This masquerade has helped the Devil convince men that he does not exist. When no man recognises, the more power he exercises. God has defined Himself as 'I am Who am,' and the Devil as 'I am who am not.'

Nowhere in Sacred Scripture do we find warrant for the popular myth of the Devil as a buffoon who is dressed like the first 'red.' Rather is he described as an angel fallen from heaven, as 'the Prince of this world,' whose business it is to tell us that there is no other world. His logic is simple: if there is no heaven there is no hell; if there is no hell, then there is no sin; if there is no sin, then there is no judge, and if there is no judgment then evil is good and good is evil. But above all these descriptions, Our Lord tells us that he will be so much like Himself that he would deceive even the elect – and certainly no devil ever seen in picture books could deceive even the elect. How will he come in this new age to win followers to his religion?

The pre-Communist Russian belief is that he will come disguised as the Great Humanitarian; he will talk peace, prosperity and plenty not as means to lead us to God, but as ends in themselves ...[8]

The third temptation in which Satan asked Christ to adore him and all the kingdoms of the world would be His, will become the temptation to have a new religion without a Cross, a liturgy without a world to come, a religion to destroy a religion, or a politics which is a religion – one that renders unto Caesar even the things that are God's.

In the midst of all his seeming love for humanity and his glib talk of freedom, he will have one great secret which he will tell to no one: he will not believe in God. Because his religion will be brotherhood without the fatherhood of God, he will deceive even the elect. He will set up a counter-church which will be the ape (copy) of the Church, because he, the Devil, is the ape (copy) of God. It will have all the notes and characteristics of the Church, but in reverse and emptied of its divine content. It will be a mystical body of the Antichrist that will in all externals resemble the mystical body of Christ.'[9]

As was mentioned in chapter four above, the antichrist is associated with a humanistic form of messianism where human beings elevate themselves to a quasi divine status as the final arbiters of

---

[8] I suspect that this is a reference to Vladimir Soloviev's, (1853-1900) 'Tale of the Antichrist.'

[9] Fulton J. Sheen, *Communism and the Conscience of the West* (Indianapolis: Bobbs-Merril Company, 1948), 24-25.

truth and falsehood, good and evil. As Judges 21:25 says, 'In those days there was no king in Israel [no ultimate authority]. Everyone did what was right in his own eyes.' As we have already seen, a number of recent Christian leaders have adverted to this tendency as diabolical in origin. 'I will not serve' was a phrase attributed to Lucifer. That contemporary attitude is a possible sign of the onset of the end times.

4] ST PAUL VI

A year before his death in 1978 St. Pope Paul VI said,

> 'There is at this time, a great turmoil in the world and in the Church, and what is in question is the faith . . . And now it comes to me to repeat the obscure phrase of Jesus in the Gospel of Luke, 'When the Son of man returns, will he find faith on earth.' There are books coming out in which the faith is in retreat on some important points, the bishops are remaining silent and these books are not found strange. In my view this is odd. I sometimes re-read the Gospel on the end of times and I notice that, at this moment, *there are emerging some signs of this end.* Are we close to the end? This is something we shall never know.'[10]

5] ST JOHN PAUL II

Cardinal Karol Józef Wojtyła (St. John Paul II) said something similar to his predecessors in Philadelphia in 1976,

> 'We are now standing in the face of the greatest historical confrontation humanity has ever experienced. I do not think that the wide circle of the American Society, or the whole wide circle of the Christian Community realise this fully. We

---

[10] Jean Guitton, *Paul VIs Secret* (Bruges: Desclée De Brouwer, 1979), 152 -153.

are now facing the final confrontation between the Church and the anti-church, between the gospel and the anti-gospel, between Christ and the antichrist. The confrontation lies within the plans of Divine Providence. It is, therefore, in God's Plan, and it must be a trial which the Church must take up, and face courageously.'[11]

In his 2005 book *Memory and Identity: Conversations at the Dawn of a Millennium* St John Paul suggested that abortion was a 'legal extermination' comparable to attempts to wipe out Jews and other groups in the 20th century. He added that the world-wide push for same sex unions was part of an ideology of evil. 'It is legitimate and necessary to ask oneself if this is not perhaps part of a new ideology of evil, perhaps more insidious and hidden, which attempts to pit human rights against the family and against man,'[12] When John Paul II talked about the final confrontation, his words could be understood in two ways. Firstly, one could argue, as I have mentioned earlier, the final confrontation refers to the whole long period between the Ascension of Jesus and his second coming. The more I have reflected on apocalyptic prophecy the more I have become aware that all the major themes such as wars, earthquakes, famines etc. are constantly present. Secondly, John Paul's words could be interpreted in a narrower sense as a reference to the shorter run-in period just before the end-times when a number of preliminary events prophesied in scriptures will have already occurred. I suspect that he had the latter understanding in mind when he spoke in America. Later in 1980 John Paul II added,

---

[11] In an address during the 1976 Eucharistic Congress in Philadelphia for the bicentennial celebration of the signing of the Declaration of Independence.

[12] (New York: Random House, 2005).

'We must be prepared to undergo great trials in the not-too-distant future; trials that will require us to be ready to give up even our lives, and a total gift of self to Christ and for Christ. Through your prayers and mine, it is possible to alleviate this tribulation, but it is no longer possible to avert it. . . .How many times has the renewal of the Church been brought about in blood! It will not be different this time.'[13]

Judging by what St. John Paul said, it would appear that we are facing into a difficult time of chastisement and purification that will be part of the final confrontation. In this context it is worth noting that Pope John Paul II said that Christian eschatology is

'An historical process which has already begun and which is moving towards fullness . . . The apocalyptic images of the eschatological discourse of Jesus concerning the end of all things must be interpreted as being symbolic. They express the precariousness of the world and the sovereign power of Christ who holds the destiny of humanity in his hands. History is moving towards its end, but Christ has given no chronological indicator. However, the attempts to predict the end of the world are illusory and misleading. Christ has assured us only that the end will not arrive before his saving work has reached its universal dimension, through the proclamation of the Gospel.'[14]

I entirely agree with St John Paul when he says, 'attempts to predict the end of the world are illusory and misleading.' In a later chapter we will see that down through Christian history many precise

---

[13] A published interview with John Paul II in the German magazine *Stimme des Glaubens*, Oct 1981.

[14] General Audience of Wednesday, April 22, 1998.

predictions have been made and all of them, without exception, have proved to be false. In this book the focus will be on the anticipatory signs of the end times which are mentioned in the Bible's apocalyptic writings. We do this with a view to seeing whether they have already been fulfilled. John Paul probably did not believe that the end of the world is coming anytime soon. After all, he spoke on numerous occasions about the coming of a new Springtime for Christianity and a civilisation of love.

CONCLUSION

In the introduction to this book there was a reference to the so called, 'Doomsday Clock' of the scientific world that sees the history of humanity in relation to a twenty four hour clock. One could also refer to a 'Doomsday Clock' of a theological kind. It began with the resurrection and the ascension of Jesus into heaven and will reach midnight when Jesus comes again. In terms of those twenty four hours where are we? Having read what inspired Church leaders have been saying over the last hundred years or so, one would have reason to suspect that we are more than two minutes from midnight. In his excellent book, *Heralds of the Second Coming*, Stephen Walford cites many interesting Marian and papal statements which speak of the immanence of the Second Coming.[15] It struck me however, that they are open to two interpretations. They could be seen as either references to an imminent, but recurring instance of a minor tribulation of a purifying kind, or to the advent of the final tribulation that will precede Christ's second coming in glory. One way or the other it seems to me that what the Marian and papal statements cited by Walford are doing is restoring a much needed eschatological dimension to Christian theology and consciousness.

---

[15] (Tacoma, WA: Angelico Press, 2013).

SEVEN

SOME RECENT SEERS AND PROPHETS ON THE END-TIMES

IN THIS CHAPTER I INTEND TO EXAMINE what some relatively modern seers have said about the second coming of Jesus. Having provided a brief biographical sketch of each person, we will go on to quote what they said. This will be done with very little comment or interpretation, in the belief that these apocalyptic prophecies speak for themselves. It is up to the reader to reflect on them in a prayerful way while asking God not only for help in understanding them but also an ability to discern if they are true in whole or in part.

1] ANNA MARIA TIAGI (1769-1837)

Anna Maria Tiagi, an Italian, was a married woman. It was alleged however that she had an adulterous affair with an older man. She became a Secular Trinitarian after experiencing a sudden religious conversion in winter 1790 while at Saint Peter's Basilica. She went on to live a very holy life. She was dedicated to the poor, esteemed by many influential people in Rome and had a reputation as a seer who experienced a series of ecstasies and prophetic visions in the course of which she foresaw the future. Here is what she said about the end times.

'God will send two punishments: one will be in the form of wars, revolutions and other evils; it shall originate on earth. The other will be sent from Heaven. There shall come over the whole earth an intense darkness lasting three days and three nights. Nothing will be seen, and the air will be laden with pestilence which will claim mainly, but not only, the enemies of religion. It will be impossible to use any man-made lighting during this darkness, except blessed candles. He, who out of curiosity, opens his window to look out, or leaves his home, will fall dead on the spot. During these three days, people should remain in their homes, pray the Rosary and beg God for mercy.

On this terrible occasion so many of these wicked men, enemies of His Church, and of their God, shall be killed by this divine scourge, that their corpses around Rome will be as numerous as the fishes, which a recent inundation of the Tiber had carried into the city. All the enemies of the Church, secret as well as known, will perish over the whole earth during that universal darkness, with the exception of some few, whom God will soon after convert. The air shall be infested by demons, who will appear under all sorts of hideous forms.

After the three days of darkness, Saints Peter and Paul, having come down from heaven, will preach throughout the world and designate a new Pope. A great light will flash from their bodies and settle upon the cardinal, the future pontiff. Then Christianity will spread throughout the world. Whole nations will join the Church shortly before the reign of the Antichrist. These conversions will be amazing. Those who survive shall have to conduct themselves well. There shall be innumerable conversions of heretics, who will return to the bosom of the Church; all will note the edifying conduct of their lives, as well as that of other Catholics. Russia, England and China will come into the Church.[1]

France will fall into frightful anarchy. The French people shall have a desperate civil war, in which old men themselves will take up arms. The political parties having exhausted their blood and their rage, without being able to arrive at any satisfactory understanding, shall at the last extremity agree by common consent to have recourse to the Holy See. Then the Pope shall send France a special legate, in order that he may examine the state of affairs and the dispositions of the people. In consequence of the information received, His Holiness himself shall nominate a most Christian king for the government of France... Religion shall be persecuted, and priests massacred Churches shall be closed, but only for a short time. The Holy Father shall be obliged to leave Rome.[2]

Anna Maria was not the only prophetic person who spoke about three days of darkness. Elizabeth Canori-Mora, Rosa-Colomba Asdente, Palma d'Oria, in Italy; Father Nectou, in Belgium; St. Hildegard, in Germany; Pere Lamy, Marie Baourdi, Marie Martel, Marie-Julie Jahenny, in France also spoke about this phenomenon. There is a well known prophecy on the internet which is attributed to St Pio of Pietrelcina (1887-1968) in which he allegedly talked about the coming three days of darkness. However, no scholar can track down a reliable source for that statement. The Capuchin

---

[1] The above is taken from the documentation for the beatification of Anna Maria Tiagi and quoted by Desmond Birch in *Trial, Tribulation & Triumph* (Goleta, CA: Queenship Publishing Company, 1996), 288-89.

[2] Ibid., 278.

Order, to which Padre Pio belonged, issued an official denial that he ever made any such prediction.[3]

2] MGR ROBERT HUGH BENSON (1871-1914)

Robert Hugh Benson, a former Anglican priest, and the son of the Archbishop of Canterbury joined the Catholic Church in 1903 and was ordained a Catholic priest the following year. Besides engaging in pastoral work he was also a writer. In 1907 he published an apocalyptic type novel entitled, *Lord of the World*.[4]

As Fr Rev. James V. Schall, S.J. explained in a review of the book[5] the hero is an English priest, Percy Franklin, who looks almost exactly like the mysterious Julian Felsenburgh, the American senator from Vermont. The senator appears as a lone and dramatic figure promising the world goodness if it consents to follow him. No one quite knows who he is or where he is from, but his voice mesmerizes. Under his leadership, East and West join up. War is abolished. Felsenburgh becomes the President of Europe, then of the world, by popular acclaim. Everyone is fascinated with him, yet still no one knows much about him. People are both riveted and frightened by the way he demands attention. Most follow him without question.

The only group who in any sense oppose him are a few loyal Catholics. The English priest is eventually called to Rome, since he has been an acute observer of the rise of Felsenburgh and his agenda. Apostasies among bishops and priests increase. The pope,

---

[3] Desmond A. Birch, *Trial, Tribulation & Triumph: Before, During and After Antichrist* (Goleta, CA: Queenship Publishing, 1996), 283-294.

[4] (Eastford, CT: Martino Fine Books, 2015). There is a good article on Wikipedia about the book.

[5] http://www.freerepublic.com/focus/f-religion/2206647/posts (Accessed 3.2.19).

John XXIV, is a good man - not unlike Pius X, who was pope when this novel was written.

Belief in God is to be replaced by belief in man. All those who oppose this doctrine are slated for extermination. With the English priest's inspiration, the pope forms a new religious order, the Order of Christ Crucified. Its members, including the pope, vow to die in the name of the faith rather than capitulate. Many do die.

The English prime minister and his wife form a sub-plot: The wife desperately wants to believe in this new world movement, but she is horrified when she sees the killings that are justified in the name of world unity. Meanwhile, the prime minister's mother is brought back to the faith by the English priest, much to the horror of the prime minister. But the wife is upset at the whole thing. Finally, to escape it all, she applies for and is granted public euthanasia. She dies not believing, but somehow knowing that what is coming with Felsenburgh is utterly horrible.

As the world comes to an end, the pope calls all the cardinals to Rome. Meantime, some English Catholics, against orders, plot to blow up the Abbey where the politicians meet. Percy Franklin, now a cardinal, along with a German cardinal, are sent back home to try to prevent this plot, which they are warned about. But word gets out. In retaliation, Felsenburgh orders that Rome be destroyed, which it is, together with the pope and all the cardinals except for the three who were not in Rome at the time. These three quickly elect the younger Englishman as the new pope, who is named Sylvester III. The old cardinal in Jerusalem dies. The German cardinal is hanged.

The last pope goes to the Holy Land, to the places associated with the last days of Christ. In a final act, Felsenburgh and all the world leaders fly in formation to destroy the remaining signs of faith on earth. In response, Sylvester and the remaining Catholics attend Mass. As they sing together the music of Benediction, i.e., the *Tantum Ergo*, the attack strikes. With that, the world ends. The last words of the novel are: 'Then this world passed, and the glory of it.' It could not be more dramatic, or more moving. *Lord of the World* has been praised by Pope Francis (November 2013) as depicting 'the spirit of the world which leads to apostasy' and it was mentioned by Pope Benedict XVI when he critiqued President George H.W. Bush's *'New World Order.'*

3] Hilaire Belloc (1870-1953)

Belloc was one of the most prolific writers in England during the early twentieth century. His Catholic faith had a strong impact on his works. In 1938 he published, *The Great Heresies*.[6] Having described historical errors in the first five chapters, he went on in the final chapter to comment on the challenges the contemporary Church will have to face. Although he was not known as a seer or prophet what he wrote is surprisingly prescient. He said,

> 'We approach the greatest moment of all. The Faith is now in the presence not of a particular heresy as in the past - the Arian, the Manichean, the Albigensian, the Mohammedan . . . The enemy which the faith now has to meet, and which may be called 'The Modern Attack,' is a wholesale assault upon the fundamentals of the faith - upon the very existence of the faith. . . The Modern Attack on the Catholic Church, the most universal that she has suffered since her foundation,

---

[6] (London: Sheed & Ward, 1938).

has so far progressed that it has already produced social, intellectual and moral forms which combined give it the savour of a religion. Though this modern attack, as I have said, is not a heresy in the old sense of the word, nor a sort of synthesis of heresies having in common a hatred of the faith, it is even more profound, and its consequences more devastating than any of these. It is essentially atheist, even when the atheism is not overtly predicated. It regards man as sufficient to himself, prayer as mere self-suggestion and - the fundamental point - God as no more than a figment of the imagination, an image of man's self thrown by man on the universe; a phantasm and no reality. . . This is the modern enemy; this is that rising flood; the greatest and what may prove to be the final struggle between the Church and the world. We must judge it principally by its fruits; and these fruits, though not yet mature, are already apparent. . . . The late Robert Hugh Benson wrote two books, each remarkable and each envisaging one of the opposite possibilities. In the first, the *Lord of the World,* he presents the picture of the Church reduced to a little wandering band, returning as it were to its origins, the Pope at the head of the Twelve - and a conclusion on the Day of Judgement. In the second he envisages the full restoration of the Catholic thing - our civilization re-established, reinvigorated, once more seated and clothed in its right mind; because in that new culture, though filled with human imperfection, the Church will have recovered her leadership of men and will inform the spirit of society with proportion and beauty once more. . . The ranks have lined up as for a battle; and though such clear division does not mean that the one or the other antagonist will conquer.'

In saying these things Belloc was echoing a number of the prophetic points made by Church leaders in a previous chapter. 'The 'quarrel' we are in right now,' said Belloc which anticipated the words of Karol Wojtytla in 1976, 'is between the Church and the anti-Church – the Church of God and the anti-God – the Church of Christ and the Anti-Christ.'

4] BLESSED ELENA AIELLO (1895 - 1961)

As her name suggests, Alena Aiello was Italian. As a young woman she became a nun and when she was older she founded a new order, The Sister Minims of The Passion of Our Lord Jesus Christ. This order was based on a similar order of Monks founded by San Francis of Paola. Sister Elena began suffering the full stigmata every Good Friday from 1923 until shortly before her death. She experienced apparitions of the Blessed Virgin Mary from 1947 until her death. These visions gifted her with the charism of prophecy when the Blessed Virgin showed her visions of the future. Here is something she said. It is not clear whether her words referred to a minor time of tribulation or the great tribulation that will precede the end times.

> Oh, what a horrible vision I see! A great revolution is going on in Rome! They are entering the Vatican. The Pope is all alone; he is praying. They are holding the Pope. They take him by force. They knock him down to the floor. They are tying him. Oh. God! Oh, God! They are kicking him. What a horrible scene! How dreadful!

> Russia will march upon all the nations of Europe, particularly Italy, and will raise her flag over the dome of St. Peter's. Italy will be severely tried by a great revolution, and Rome will be

purified in blood for its many sins, especially those of impurity. The flock is about to be dispersed and the Pope will suffer greatly.'[7]

On Good Friday April 16th 1954, Blessed Elena Aiello received this prophetic word that does seem to refer to the end-times,

'Clouds with lightening rays of fire and a tempest of fire will pass over the whole world and the punishment will be the most terrible ever known in the history of mankind. It will last 70 hours [three days]. The wicked will be crushed and eliminated. Many will be lost because they will feel the force of light over darkness. The hours of darkness are near.'[8]

5] SR LÚCIA DE JESUS ROSA DOS SANTOS OF FÁTIMA (1907-2005)
Lúcia de Jesus Rosa dos Santos, O.C.D., also known as Lúcia of Fátima, was a Portuguese Carmelite nun. At the age of nine, she was sent with her cousins, Francisco and Jacinta Matos to shepherd the sheep as usual. It was then that they received a visit from the Virgin in Cova de Iria. In adult life Lucia became a religious. She lived firstly in convents in Spain and from 1946 onwards in Portugal. As a grown woman she received many prophetic messages from Our Lady and from Our Lord. Some of them concerned the end times. As I reported in *Prophecy: Truth for Today Light for Tomorrow*, she said that the battle between good and evil during the final confrontation, in which we are already engaged, would centre on the family. In 1957 Lucia was interviewed by a Fr. Fuentes. On that occasion she said that she felt that the Lord was preparing the world for the end. Apparently Our Lady had said to

---

[7] Desmond Birch in Trial, Tribulation & Triumph, op. cit., 392.

[8] Desmond Birch in Trial, Tribulation & Triumph, op. cit., 293.

her, 'The last aids that God will give to the world for its salvation are the Holy Rosary and my Immaculate Heart.' He mentioned that Sr Lucia was given to understand that the world was living in the last phase of the end times for two reasons. Firstly, because the world was going through a decisive battle in which there would be no room for sitting on the fence; people would have to choose between either God or Satan. And, secondly, that whenever Our Lord decides to chastise the world, he first uses every means to save humanity, and seeing that this fails, he sends the Blessed Virgin and Mother as the last chance of salvation.[9]

6] St Faustina Kowalska (1905-1938)

Born in Poland, Helena Kowalska joined a convent in Warsaw, at the age of twenty. She was transferred to Płock, and was later moved to Vilnius in Lithuania where she met Father Michał Sopoćko who not only became her confessor but who also supported her devotion to the Divine Mercy. As a result of many visions and locutions she wrote her Diary which not only contains a number of prophecies, it also contains apocalyptic material. Her prediction about a forthcoming 'spark from Poland' (*Diary 1732*) who would prepare the world for the Second Coming of Christ is one of her best known private revelations. Many people believe that it was referring to the pontificate of St John Paul II, others think it was a reference to Faustina herself. But it could also be argued that it referred to the remarkable St Maximilian Kolbe (1894-1941). After all, she had been told by the Lord, 'You will prepare the world for My final coming' (*Diary 429*). It was John Paul who approved of Faustina's writings, wrote an encyclical on *Divine Mercy* (1980) which was influenced by her message, and instituted Divine Mercy Sunday. Providentially, John Paul died on the vigil of Divine Mercy

---

[9] Stephen Walford, *Heralds of the Second Coming* Tacoma: Angelico Press, 2013),74 .

Sunday 2005, and was beatified and canonised on Divine Mercy Sundays 2011 and 2014 respectively. It would probably be true to say that John Paul regarded his fellow Pole as the greatest prophet of the 20th century. At this point we will examine a number of Faustina's statements about the Second Coming. All the references are to the numbered paragraphs in her *Diary*.[10]

A] VOCATION TO BE AN APOCALYPTIC PROPHET
In 1935 the Lord said to Faustina,

> 'You will prepare the world for My final coming.' These words moved me deeply, and although I pretended not to hear them , I understood them very well and had no doubt about them' *(Diary 429)*.

In 1936, Faustina reported that the Mother of God had spoken these words to her.

> 'Oh, how pleasing to God is the soul that follows faithfully the inspirations of His grace! I gave the Saviour to the world; as for you, you have to speak to the world about His great mercy and prepare the world for the Second Coming of Him who will come, not as a merciful Saviour, but as a just Judge. Oh, how terrible is that day! Determined is the day of justice, the day of divine wrath. The angels tremble before it. Speak to souls about this great mercy while it is still the time for [granting] mercy. If you keep silent now, you will be answering for a great number of souls on that terrible day. Fear nothing. Be faithful to the end. I sympathise with you' *(Diary 635)*.

---

[10] *Diary of St Maria Faustina Kowalska* (Stockbridge: Marian Press, 2015).

Coming toward the end of her relatively short life St Faustina received this message.

> 'Today I heard the words: In the Old Covenant I sent prophets wielding thunderbolts to my people. Today I am sending you with my mercy to the people of the whole world. I do not want to punish aching mankind, but I desire to heal it, pressing it to my merciful heart. I use punishment when they themselves force me to do so. My hand is reluctant to take hold of the sword of justice. Before the Day of Justice I am sending the day of mercy' *(Diary 1588)*.

B] THE APOCALYPTIC MESSAGE

In 1934 the Lord instructed St Faustina to report this remarkable revelation.

> 'Write this: before I come as the Just Judge, I am coming first as the King of Mercy. Before the day of justice arrives, there will be given to people a sign in the heavens of this sort: All light in the heavens will be extinguished, and there will be great darkness over the whole earth. Then the sign of the cross will be seen in the sky, and from the openings where the hands and the feet of the Saviour were nailed will come forth great lights which will light up the earth for a period of time. This will take place shortly before the last day' *(Diary 83)*.

As has been noted above, this notion of a world-wide darkness for a number of days is a theme that was mentioned by a number of other prophets and seers. St Faustina returned to the inter-relationship of the justice and mercy of God in another revelation.

'Jesus looked at me and said, 'Souls perish in spite of My bitter Passion. I am giving them the last hope of salvation; that is, the Feast of My Mercy. If they will not adore My mercy, they will perish for all eternity. Secretary of My mercy, write, tell souls about this great mercy of mine, because the awful day, the day of My justice, is near.' *(Diary 965).*

C] HOW TO RESPOND

St Faustina was told in a number of revelations how people should respond.

'Write down these words, My daughter. Speak to the world about My mercy; let all mankind recognise My unfathomable mercy. It is a sign for the end times; after it will come the day of justice. While there is still time, let them have recourse to the fount of My mercy; let them profit from the Blood and Water which gushed forth for them' *(Diary 848).*

On another occasion the Lord spoke these consoling and challenging words.

'Let the greatest sinners place their trust in My mercy. They have the right before others to trust in the abyss of My mercy. My daughter, write about My mercy towards tormented souls. Souls that make an appeal to My mercy delight Me. To such souls I grant even more graces than they ask. I cannot punish even the greatest sinner if he makes an appeal to My compassion, but on the contrary, I justify him in My unfathomable and inscrutable mercy. Write: before I come as a just Judge, I first open wide the door of My mercy. He who refuses to pass through the door of My mercy must pass through the door of My justice' *(Diary 1146)*

Finally St Faustina wrote these practical and illuminating words about performing at least one merciful act a day in preparation for the end of days.

> 'Such deeds can easily be carried out by anyone, even the very poorest. For there are three ways of performing an act of mercy: the merciful word, by forgiving and by comforting; secondly, if you can offer no word, then pray – that too is mercy; and thirdly, deeds of mercy. And when the Last Day comes, we shall be judged from this, and on this basis we shall receive the eternal verdict' *(Diary 1158).*

C] ST FAUSTINA'S APOCALYPTIC PRAYER

St Faustina concluded her fifth notebook with this beautiful eschatological prayer.

> 'I do not know, O Lord, at what hour you will come. And so I keep constant watch and listen as your chosen bride, knowing that you like to come unexpectedly, yet, a pure heart will sense you from afar, O Lord. I wait for you, Lord, in calm and silence, and with invincible desire. I feel that my love for you is changing into fire, and that it will rise up to heaven like a flame at life's end, and then all my wishes will be fulfilled.
>
> Come then, at last, my most sweet Lord and take my thirsting heart there, to your home in the lofty regions of heaven, where your eternal life perdures. Life on this earth is but an agony, as my heart feels it is created for the heights. The lowlands of this life hold no interest, for my homeland is in heaven – this I firmly believe.' *(Diary 1589).*

CONCLUSION

The people quoted in this chapter not only have a reputation for wisdom and holiness, their private revelations have been approved by the Church. That said, no Catholic is bound to accept them as being true. Happily, none of them claim to have any exact idea when the end times will come. All they assert is the fact that we are living in the age of mercy which will be followed by the age of justice. Anyone who has received divine forgiveness during their lifetime will have nothing to fear.

In Jm 5: 7-10 we read, 'So be patient, brothers and sisters, until the Lord's return. Think of how the farmer waits for the precious fruit of the ground and is patient for it until it receives the early and late rains. You also be patient and strengthen your hearts, for the Lord's return is near. Do not grumble against one another, brothers and sisters, so that you may not be judged. See, the judge stands before the gates!'

EIGHT

THE UNRELIABILITY OF PRECISE AND SPECIFIC APOCALYPTIC PREDICTIONS

APOCALYPTIC WRITING HAS BEEN A CONSTANT FEATURE of Church history. Time and time again apocalyptic predictions were proven to be mistaken. There are many examples. In the second century Montanus and his two female collaborators Pricilla and Maximilla claimed to be prophets. The three of them spoke during ecstatic visions and urged their followers to fast and to pray, so that they too might share these revelations. They forecast many things. For example, Maximilla warned of an impending time of warfare and anarchy - which never came to pass. The trio firmly, but mistakenly, believed that the end of the world was approaching soon. In the third century St. Hippolytus, who had a big influence on our second Eucharistic prayer, used a combination of maths and exegesis to predict that the end of the world would take place in 500 AD. In the fourth century St. Hilary of Poitier was credited with fixing the end of the world at 365 A.D. In the same century St Martin of Tours, a disciple of St. Hilary, apparently shared his master's conviction that the Antichrist was already living and calculated the world's end would occur around 400 A.D.

VINCENT FERRER THE ANGEL OF JUDGMENT

Even before his birth at Valentia in Spain in 1350, it seemed that Vincent Ferrer was predestined by God to accomplish great things. A Dominican said prophetically to his father, 'I congratulate you William. In a few days you will have a son who will become a prodigy of learning and sanctity. . . The world will resound with the fame of his wondrous deeds; he will fill heaven with joy and hell with terror. He will put on the habit which I wear, and will be received in the Church with universal joy as one of its first apostles.' Vincent did join the Dominicans at the age of twenty two, became a doctor of theology, and began to teach and preach. During this time he wrote a *Treatise on the Spiritual Life* which mainly had the members of the Dominican Order in mind. It is a succinct, practical, and demanding summary of how to live a life of Christian perfection. In spite of his obvious holiness of life, Vincent was accused of heresy because he questioned the prevailing view when he taught that Judas may have gone to purgatory rather than hell. The charge was dismissed by his mentor, the anti-pope Benedict XIII, who burned the Inquisition's dossier and made Vincent his confessor.

During a time of serious illness sometime between 1396-9, Vincent had a vision of Christ standing between Sts. Dominic and Francis, who told him to go forth and preach repentance and the immanence of the end times. Vincent had good reason to believe that the end times were close at hand. The continent of Europe was in deep trouble.

Firstly, there was a little ice age in the 14th century when the weather got a good deal colder and had an adverse effect on agriculture. For example, the Baltic Sea froze over in 1303, 1306 and 1307, something never before recorded. Secondly, the great famine of (1315-17) had a devastating effect and was marked by extreme levels of crime, disease, death and even cannibalism. Thirdly, the black death (1347-51), had ravaged every country, including Spain, and resulted in the loss of between twenty and twenty five million people, i.e. a third of the population. The mortality rate was erratic, ranging from one fifth in some places to nine tenths or almost total elimination in others. There were six more waves of plague between 1350 and 1400. During the great famine between 1301 and 1325, life expectancy was 29.84, while during the black death, and subsequent plagues between 1348 and 1375, it went down to only 17.33. Fourthly, the hundred years war (1337-1453) between England and France not only led to the martyrdom of St Joan of Arc (1412-1431), it had a widespread destructive and destabilising effect. Fifthly, because so many people had died as a result of bubonic plague and violence, the economy declined due to a lack of workers. Sixthly, the Church was convulsed by the great schism which lasted from 1378 to 1417, and it was undermined by the heresies of people like John Wycliffe (1330-84) and John Huss (1372-1415). These scandalous situations, compromised ecclesiastical authority, divided the faithful, and weakened spirituality. Clement VI, was the Avignon Pope during the Black Death. Although he himself was no saint he had this to say about his fellow churchmen, 'What can you preach to the people? If on humility, you yourselves are the proudest of the world, puffed up, pompous and sumptuous in luxuries. If on poverty, you are so covetous that all the benefices of the world are not enough for you. If on chastity - but we will be silent on this, for God knows what each man does and how many of you satisfy your lusts.'

Vincent responded to this dire situation by conducting one of the most extraordinary missionary outreaches in the history of the Church. For twenty years, he travelled tirelessly the length and breadth of Europe preaching in places such as Marseilles, Geneva, Lausanne, Bologna and Freiburg. Henry V, King of England, being then at Caen in Normandy, entreated the saint to extend his zeal to that province. He did so; and Normandy and Brittany were the theatre of the apostle's labours for the two last years of his life.

Vincent felt that the Church of his time was corrupt and in urgent need of reform. He wrote,

> 'There never existed in the world so much pomp and vanity, so much impurity, as at the present day; to find in the world's history an epoch so criminal, we must go back to the days of Noah and the universal deluge. The inns in the cities and villages are filled with persons of abandoned character; they are so numerous that the entire world is infected by them . . . Avarice and usury increase under the disguised name of contracts. Simony reigns among the clergy, envy among the religious. Gluttony prevails to such an extent in every rank of social life that the fasts of Lent, the vigils and Ember Days, are no longer observed . . . In a word, vice is held in such great honour that those who prefer the service of God to that of the world are held up to scorn as useless and unworthy members of society.'[1]

Apparently St Vincent identified in a personal way with two verses in Rev 14:6-7 which say, 'I saw another angel flying in midair, and he had the eternal gospel to proclaim to those who live on the earth - to every nation, tribe, language and people. He said in a loud voice, 'Fear God and give him glory, because the hour of his judgment has come. Worship him who made the heavens, the earth, the sea and the springs of water.' In his book *The End of the Present World*, Fr. Charles Arminjon, recounted how St Vincent Ferrer

---

[1] Andrew Pradel, O.P., *St Vincent Ferrer: The Angel of Judgment* (Rockford: Tan, 2000), 48-49.

declared, 'I am the angel of the Apocalypse, the angel of judgment.'
When the people took offence at his making such a pretentious
claim he is reported to have responded, 'Do not take scandal at
my words. You will see with your own eyes that I am what I say.
Go to the gate of St. Paul, at the edge of the city and you will find
a dead woman. Bring her to me, and I shall raise her to life, as proof
of what St. John said to me.' The dead woman was found as Vincent
had foretold. When her body was brought to him he said, 'Woman,
in the name of God, I command you to rise.' Immediately she sat
up. Vincent then went on to say, 'For the honour of God and the
salvation of all these people, say whether I am really the angel of
the Apocalypse, entrusted with proclaiming to all the approach of
the last judgment.' The woman replied, 'You are that angel, truly
you are.' Then Vincent responded, 'Do you prefer to remain alive,
or do you desire to die once more?' 'I should willingly live,' replied
the woman. In the event she lived for many more years.[2] With this
in mind we can say with assurance that when St Vincent spoke
about the end times he did so with unique insight and authority.[3]

As an apocalyptic preacher St Vincent spoke mainly about sin,
repentance, death, judgment, heaven and hell. For example in one
lengthy sermon delivered on the second Sunday of Advent he said,

> 'Three of the greatest and most terrible afflictions are shortly
> to come upon mankind: first, the affliction of Antichrist, a
> man but a diabolical one; second, the destruction by fire of
> the terrestrial world; third, the universal judgment. And with
> these tribulations the world will come to an end. Therefore,

---

[2] (Manchester, New Hampshire: Sophia Institute Press, 2008), 29-30.

[3] Charles Arminjon, *The End of the Present World & the Mysteries of the Future Life*
(Manchester, NH: Sophia Institute Press, 2008), 29-30.

according to the rule of divine Providence, before these three, there will be warning signs in the heavens, in the sun and in the moon and in the stars.'[4]

No wonder his preaching made such a profound impression on the people. Furthermore, it was reinforced and validated by the fact that he worked countless miracles.

He also made a number of accurate prophesies. Among them was one that foretold a time when the Holy Spirit would be widely distributed among several men, who would bring about the renewal of the Church and the conversion of unbelievers. This notion is reminiscent of what Joachim of Fiore had said about the advent of the age of the Spirit. St. Vincent de Paul referred to this prophecy on no less than three occasions. He wondered if perchance the establishment of his own congregation was part of the fulfilment of Ferrer's prediction. Although one cleric, at the time, referred to Vincent de Paul as the new Vincent Ferrer, I would suspect that the Jesuits were more likely to have been the kind of Order he had in mind because they would spearhead the Counter Reformation and renewal of the Church. Vincent Ferrer once said to a novice, Alphonso Borgia, 'You will become pope and will canonise me.' And years later that novice, then Pope Callixtus III, did exactly that. Vincent also told St. Bernardine of Siena that he Bernardine would be canonised before himself and so it happened.

Needless to say, Vincent's prophetic gifts added gravitas to his apocalyptic prophecy. He was so convinced that he was living in

---

[4] The third of the sermons given on the second Sunday in Advent; on the last judgment in *Angel of the Judgment: A Life of Vincent Ferrer*, by S.M.C., (Notre Dame: Ave Maria Press, 1954), 102-117. For the full text see Appendix A below.

the end times that on July 7th 1412 he wrote a long letter about the subject to Pope Benedict XIII in Avignon, for his discernment. He said to the Pontiff,

> 'I hold the opinion, which I think to be well founded, though not sufficiently proven for me to preach it, that nine years have already elapsed since the birth of Antichrist. But this I do preach with certitude and security, the Lord confirming my word by many signs, that in an exceedingly short time will come the reign of Antichrist and the end of the world.'

It is worth our while to quote one extended extract from Vincent's letter to the Pope.

> 'Since then the aforesaid religious (i.e., Vincent) has been travelling for thirteen years over the world, and is still journeying, preaching every day and in many labours, and though he is now an old man, more than sixty years old, he still holds this conclusion as most certain.

> The same conclusion is also shown me by another revelation which I heard from a certain holy and devout man - as I consider him. When I was preaching in the province of Lombardy for the first time eleven years ago, there came to me from Tuscany a man sent, as he said, by certain most holy hermits of great austerity of life, to tell me that a divine revelation had been made to several of these men that the birth of Antichrist had already occurred, and must be announced to the world so that the faithful might prepare themselves for so dreadful a combat, and so they had sent the aforesaid hermit to me that I might tell the world. If then, as appears from these revelations, it is true that Antichrist had

already completed nine years of his accursed life, then it follows that my conclusion is also true.

Another clear revelation which I heard while in Piedmont, told me by a Venetian merchant on whose word I can rely, confirms this conclusion. He was beyond the seas in a certain convent of the Friars Minor, and was attending Vespers on a certain feast day. At the end of Vespers, two little novices, according to their custom, singing the *'Benedicamus Domino,'* were visibly rapt in ecstasy for a considerable period of time. At length they cried out together: 'Today, at this hour, Antichrist, the destroyer of the world is born.' This struck those present with fear and amazement, and among those who actually heard, it was the Venetian who told me of the occurrence. When I questioned him and made enquiries about this event, I found that it happened nine years previously, and so this is further corroboration of what I have already said.

This same conclusion is further borne out by many other revelations made to many other devout and spiritual persons. For, travelling as I do, through many regions, provinces, kingdoms, cities and towns, many devout and spiritual persons come to me, referring with certitude to the coming of Antichrist and the end of the world, which they have received in many and very diverse revelations, and in all of these there is the greatest concord.

Innumerable demons, forced to a confession of the truth have said the same thing. In many parts of the world, I have seen many persons possessed by the devil, who were brought to one of the priests of our company for exorcism. When the priest began to exorcise them they spoke openly of the time of Antichrist, in accordance with what has already been said, crying out loudly and terribly so that all the bystanders could hear them, and declaring that they were forced by Christ and against their own will and malice, to reveal to men the truth as given above, so that they might save themselves by true penance. These revelations have the effect of leading to contrition and penance the numerous Christians standing round. But when the demons are questioned, or even conjured to tell the truth of the birth place of Antichrist, they will not reveal it.

From all that has been said above, I hold the opinion, which I think to be well founded, though not sufficiently proven for me to preach it, that nine years have already elapsed since the birth of Antichrist. But this I do preach with certitude and security, the Lord confirming my word by many signs, that in an exceedingly short time will come the reign of Antichrist and the end of the world.'

Not surprisingly, Vincent also spoke about the end times in the course of his preaching. For example there is a lengthy and interesting homily extant which he preached for the 2nd Sunday of Advent on Luke 21:25-28. It is entitled, 'The End of the World.'[5] In another of his sermons, which he preached in Castile, in 1411, he said,

'The end of the world cannot be far distant, and the kingdom

---

[5] https://www.svfsermons.org/A061_Last%20Judgment.htm (Accessed 30 July 2019).

of God is at hand. Has not our Lord himself said that the bearing of the fig-tree foreshadows the coming Summer? Behold, then, the fig-tree of the Christian people. Each day records its reconciliation, and we witness souls forgetting and forgiving the greatest injuries. The delicate, the sensual and the vicious do penance. Obstinate sinners are converted and frequently approach the sacraments. Nor is the Jewish fig-tree any longer barren, for we see it daily producing its abundant and choicest fruits in every city in Spain.'[6]

Surely, it is significant that nearly 600 years after his death, the apocalypse Vincent preached has not come to pass. Perhaps his prophecy about the threefold afflictions to come was averted as a result of his effective evangelisation, the repentance of many people, and the intercession of Our Lady. Vincent himself said in a homily he delivered on the second Sunday of Advent on the subject of the last judgment,

'we know that when any great and heavy affliction is about to come on the world, often some warning sign is shown in the sky or in the upper air. And this happens by the mercy of God, so that people forewarned of impending tribulation by means of these signs, through prayer and good works, may obtain in the tribunal of mercy a reversal of the sentence passed against them by God the judge in the heavenly courts.'

Even so, he did state with great assurance that THE antichrist had been born during his own lifetime. In spite of his subjective

---

[6] Quoted by Andrew Pradel, O.P., in St Vincent Ferrer: *The Angel of Judgment* (Rockford, Il: Tan, 2000), 86.

conviction based on private revelation to himself and others he seemed to be mistaken.

I think that Ferrer's apocalyptic views are very instructive. Although he had good reason, to think that the end of the world was near for a number of reasons; the dire state of Europe at the time, reading the signs of the times; credible revelations given to himself and others, the many confirming miracles he himself performed, and the countless conversions he witnessed. Nevertheless he was mistaken. As historian Louis Salembier observed in *The Great Schism of the West*, 'seers arose on all sides, and their visions gained such an influence and a circulation as had been unknown before . . . In some of the gravest sermons reliance was put upon these baseless predictions.' It can be said in passing, that it is an ironic fact that in chapters twelve and thirteen of his influential *Treatise on the Spiritual Life*, Vincent warned his readers against the temptation to seek private revelations. He wrote,

> 'Have no desire to procure by prayer, meditation or any other good work, what are called revelations, or spiritual experiences, beyond what happens in the ordinary course of things . . . It is to punish this evil desire that God abandons the soul and permits it to fall into the illusions and temptations of the devil, who seduces it, and represents to it false visions and delusive revelations.'

Is it any different today? I don't think so. As a result, I am very sceptical when anyone claims that the biblical criteria for discerning the beginning of the end-times, have been met. In this connection it is good to remind ourselves of these words in Mt 24:3-7, 'As Jesus was sitting on the Mount of Olives, the disciples came to him privately. 'Tell us,' they said, 'when will this happen, and what will be the sign of your coming and of the end of the age?' Jesus answered: 'Watch out that no one deceives you. For many will come in my name, claiming, 'I am the Christ,' and will deceive many. You will hear of wars and rumours of wars, but see to it that you are not alarmed. Such things must happen, but the end is still to come.' Commenting on these words Pope Benedict XVI said in a homily entitled, 'On the coming of the Son of Man,'

> 'Jesus does not describe the end of the world and when he uses apocalyptic images he does not conduct himself like a 'visionary.' On the contrary, he wants to take away the curiosity of his disciples in every age about dates and predictions and wishes instead to give them a key to a deep, essential reading, and above all to indicate the right path to take, today and tomorrow, to enter into eternal life. Everything passes – the Lord tells us – but God's Word does not change, and before this Word each of us is responsible for his conduct. It is on this basis that we will be judged.' [7]

SOME FALSE DOOMSDAY PREDICTIONS
There has been no shortage of modern day apocalyptic predictions. Here are three of many possible examples.

• Charles Taze Russell (1852-1916) founder of the Jehovah's Witnesses maintained that Christ had returned invisibly in 1874, and that he had been ruling from the heavens since that date. He predicted that a period known as the 'Gentile Times' would end in 1914, and that Christ would take power of Earth's affairs at that time.

---

[7] Saint Peter's Square, Sunday, 18 November 2012. http://w2.vatican.va/conent/benedict-xvi/en/angelus/2012/documents/hf_ben-xvi_ang_20121118.html

- In the 19th century the Millerites were the followers of the teachings of William Miller (1782–1849) founder of the Seventh Day Adventists, who in 1833 first shared publicly his belief that the Second Advent of Jesus Christ would occur in roughly the year 1843–1844.

- In May 1980, televangelist and presidential candidate Pat Robertson startled and alarmed many when he informed his '700 Club' TV show audience around the world that he knew when the world would end. 'I guarantee you by the end of 1982 there is going to be a judgement on the world.'

- According to God's Church minister Ronald Weinland, the end times should have come by now. His book *2008: God's Final Witness* which was published in 2006 states that hundreds of millions of people would die, and by the end of 2006, 'there will be a maximum time of two years remaining before the world will be plunged into the worst time of all human history. By the fall of 2008, the United States will have collapsed as a world power, and no longer exist as an independent nation.'

- In 2001 American Christian radio host Harold Camping stated that the so-called Rapture and Judgment Day would take place on May 21st 2011, and that the end of the world would take place five months later on October 21, 2011. The Rapture, in a specific tradition of pre-millennial theology, is the taking up into heaven of God's elect...

Rather than doing any good, I suspect that apocalyptic predictions of this nature bring Christianity, and the whole notion of apocalyptic prophecy into disrepute. I feel that the second coming is still far off because many people still have to hear the Gospel, and because the conversion of the Jews to Jesus Christ as their promised messiah has not yet fully taken place.

CONCLUSION

Fr Raniero Cantalamessa, the Papal Preacher, spoke about the end times in a 2006 homily. Among other things he said,

> 'We must, I think, completely change the attitude with which we listen to these Gospels that speak of the end of the world and the return of Christ. We must no longer regard as a punishment and a veiled threat that which the Scriptures call 'the blessed hope' of Christians, that is, the return of our Lord Jesus Christ (Tit 2:13). The mistaken idea we have of God must be corrected. The recurrent talk about the end of the world which is often engaged in by those with a distorted religious sentiment, has a devastating effect on many people. It reinforces the idea of a God who is always angry, ready to vent his wrath on the world. But this is not the God of the Bible which a psalm describes as 'merciful and gracious, slow to anger and abounding in steadfast love, who will not always accuse or keep his anger forever... because he knows that we are made of dust' (Ps 103:8-14).'[8]

It was noted in a previous chapter that St. John Paul II believed that we are caught up in the final confrontation, and that we are living in the end times. However, we have no idea when the second coming of Jesus will take place.

---

[8] Commentary Nov. 17th, 2006 on the readings for 33rd Sunday in Ordinary Time (b) Daniel 12:1-3; Hebrews 10:11-14, 18; Mark 13:24-32.

Surely, Fr. Cantalamessa is right. Instead of worrying about when the world will end, Christians should seek first the kingdom of God and his righteousness by growing in personal holiness and by doing God's will in all things, especially by carrying out the great command of love, e.g., by evangelising all those who do not yet know the Lord Jesus and his merciful love. We should live each day as if were our last. As Acts 1:7 says, 'It is not for you to know times and seasons that have been set by the Father's own authority.'

NINE

POPES JOHN PAUL II AND BENEDICT XVI ON THE FUNDAMENTAL OPTION[1]

CHRISTIANS BELIEVE THAT FOLLOWING THE END OF THE WORLD, as we know it, there will be the general or last judgement. It is referred to in the scriptures. In Rev 20:11-12 we read, 'Then I saw a great white throne and him who was seated on it. From his presence earth and sky fled away, and no place was found for them. And I saw the dead, great and small, standing before the throne, and books were opened. Then another book was opened, which is the book of life. And the dead were judged by what was written in the books, according to what they had done.' People and nations will be judged by their attitude to Jesus Christ and the love they showed during our lives, e.g. by exercising the corporal works of mercy.[2] As Mt 13:40-3 tells us, 'Just as the weeds are collected and burned up with fire, so will it be at the end of the age. The Son of Man will send his angels, and they will collect out of his kingdom all causes of sin and all evildoers, and they will throw them into the furnace of fire, where there will be weeping and gnashing of teeth. Then the righteous will shine like the sun in the kingdom of their Father. Let anyone with ears listen!' During

---

[1] This is a modified version of an article I wrote, entitled, 'The Fundamental Option Papal Disparity?' in the *The Furrow* (Feb 2013): 101-107.

[2] Feed the hungry, shelter the homeless, clothe the naked, visit the sick and imprisoned, bury the dead, and give alms to the poor.

the last century the question has been repeatedly asked, how many people will be saved, a minority or the majority?[3] Saints, theologians, and even popes have offered different answers. This chapter will focus mainly on the apparently different replies of Popes John Paul II and Benedict XVI.

TWO VIEWS

A few years ago I had lunch with Dr. Ralph Martin, a lay man who lectures in Sacred Heart seminary in Detroit, broadcasts regularly on EWTN, and is the author of a number of influential books. In the course of our conversation he suddenly asked me whether I had read Pope Benedict's Encyclical *Spe Salvi* (Hope of Salvation) which deals with the four last things, namely, death, judgment, heaven and hell. I said that I had. Then he asked me what I thought of it. I responded by saying that I was surprised by what Pope Benedict had said about the fundamental option and that it seemed to differ from what John Paul II had written about it. Ralph said that he agreed with my assessment.

More recently, Martin's doctoral thesis was published. It is entitled, *Will Many be Saved? What Vatican II Actually Teaches and its Implications for the New Evangelisation.*[4] In an extended footnote on page 284, he says that it is unfortunate that certain remarks of Benedict XVI seem to support a rather modern notion of the universality of salvation which has been propounded in differing ways by some notable theologians such as Karl Rahner, S.J., Hans Urs von Balthasar and St. Edith Stein (Teresa Benedicta of the Cross). Martin is suspicious of that point of view, if for no other

---

[3] For a very good summary see Avery Dulles, S.J., 'Who Can be Saved?' *First Things* (Feb 2008).

[4] (Grand Rapids: Eerdmans, 2012).

reason than the fact that it doesn't seem to rhyme with what Jesus said, 'Enter through the narrow gate. For wide is the gate and broad is the road that leads to destruction, and many enter through it. But small is the gate and narrow the road that leads to life' (Mt 7: 12-13). Nevertheless Pope Benedict propounds a relatively modern attitude to the likelihood of salvation, especially in pars, 45-47 of *Spe Salvi*.[5] They imply that on the last day, when Christ will come again as the just Judge, perhaps only a few really evil people will be destined for hell and virtually everybody else will go to heaven, albeit, via purgatory. Martin concluded by saying in his book that Pope Benedict would do well to clarify his views.

As a result of talking to Ralph Martin and reading his book, I decided to think about this contentious issue. The fact that there is a possible disparity between what the two Pontiffs have said about the fundamental option mirrors a controversy in contemporary theology. In an article entitled, 'The Population of Hell, ' the late Cardinal Avery Dulles, S.J., said that on the one hand, 'Several studies published by Catholics early in the twentieth century concluded that there was a virtual consensus among the Fathers of the Church and the Catholic theologians of later ages to the effect that the majority of humankind go to eternal punishment in hell.' On the other hand he noted that, 'About the middle of the twentieth century, there seems to be a break in the tradition. Since then a number of influential theologians have favoured the view that all human beings may or do eventually attain salvation.'[6] Anglican theologian Richard Bauckham said something very similar, 'The history of the doctrine of universal salvation is a remarkable one. Until the nineteenth century almost all Christian

---

[5] *First Things* (May 2003).

[6] Ralph Martin, *Will Many Be Saved*, op. cit., 130

theologians taught the reality of the eternal torment of hell . . .
Since 1800 this situation has entirely changed and no traditional
Christian doctrine has been so widely abandoned as that of eternal
punishment . . . salvation is now so widely accepted . . . that many
theologians assume it virtually without argument.'[7] The apparent
differences between the two Pontiffs not only mirrors those
differing views they raise two interrelated problems, one to do with
the authority of papal statements and the other about an important
spiritual truth.

Let us look firstly at the issue of papal authority. Leaving aside the
rare occasions when Popes solemnly declare and promulgate an
ex cathedra dogmatic teaching on faith or morals, they often issue
different kinds of pronouncements such as Apostolic Exhortations,
Letters, Constitutions, Declarations, and Papal Encyclicals. As
part of the ordinary *magisterium* of the Church, some of these
publications have more authority than others. For example, in spite
of the fact that Paul VI's Apostolic Declaration *Evangelii Nuntiandi*
(Evangelisation in the Modern World) has had considerable
influence on the understanding of evangelisation in the Catholic
Church, Pope John Paul's encyclical, *Redemptoris Missio* (The
Mission of the Redeemer), on much the same subject, would have
more magisterial authority. Writing about the authority of such
letters, Pope Pius XII said in par. 20 of his encyclical *Humani Generis*
(Concerning some false opinions threatening to undermine the
foundations of Catholic Doctrine),

'If the Supreme Pontiffs in their official documents purposely
pass judgment on a matter up to that time under dispute, it

---

[7] Richard Bauckham, 'Universalism: an Historical Survey,' *Themelios* 4.2
(September 1978): 47–54.

is obvious that that matter, according to the mind and will of the Pontiffs, cannot be any longer considered a question open to discussion among theologians.'

THE FUNDAMENTAL OPTION

Now we can address the issue of spiritual truth. I first heard about the notion of the fundamental option just before my ordination in 1971. Two years later it was described by German moral theologian Joseph Fuchs, S.J. in a chapter entitled 'Basic Freedom and Morality' in his book *Human Values and Christian Morality.*[8] Apparently Fuchs was influenced by the anthropology of his colleague Karl Rahner, S.J., especially his notion of fundamental freedom. Every genuine Christian has experienced a basic conversion to the Lord which is weakened or strengthened by subsequent choices. If my memory serves me correctly, proponents of the fundamental option argued that even if a person committed a mortal sin, e.g., as a result of adultery, that choice would not necessarily change the person's deep down orientation towards truth, love and ultimately God. In other words no single act by itself is enough to merit eternal punishment in hell unless that act is of sufficient depth and seriousness to constitute a fundamental reversal of the conversion experience. So some people have argued that although a sin might be grave it might not necessarily be mortal if it doesn't change a person's fundamental option, e.g., as a result of wilful apostasy.

JOHN PAUL II ON THE FUNDAMENTAL OPTION

In his Post Synodal Apostolic Exhortation *Reconciliatio et Paenitentia* (Reconciliation and Penance), Pope John Paul II seemed to endorse a view previously propounded in par. 10 of his *Persone Humane*, which was a declaration on certain problems of sexual

---

[8] (Dublin: Gill & Macmillan, 1973).

ethics which was published by the Sacred Congregation for the
Doctrine of the Faith in 1975. He said in par. 17,

> 'Care will have to be taken not to reduce mortal sin to an act
> of 'fundamental option' - as is commonly said today - against
> God, intending thereby an explicit and formal contempt for
> God or neighbour. For mortal sin exists also when a person
> knowingly and willingly, for whatever reason, chooses some-
> thing gravely disordered. In fact, such a choice already
> includes contempt for the divine law, a rejection of God's love
> for humanity and the whole of creation; the person turns
> away from God and loses charity. *Thus the fundamental
> orientation can be radically changed by individual acts* (my italics).
> Clearly there can occur situations which are very complex
> and obscure from a psychological viewpoint and which have
> an influence on the sinner's subjective culpability. But from a
> consideration of the psychological sphere one cannot proceed
> to the construction of a theological category, which is what
> the 'fundamental option' precisely is, understanding it in
> such a way that it objectively changes or casts doubt upon
> the traditional concept of mortal sin.'

This quotation makes it pretty obvious that John Paul II rejected
the fundamental option's distinction between grave and mortal
sin. He returned to this subject in a more authoritative way in pars
65-68 of his encyclical *Veritatis Splendor* (Splendour of the Truth).
Having outlined the arguments of those who think that rather than
being a gravely sinful act, mortal sin is the result of changing one's
fundamental option, the Pope wrote,

> 'According to the logic of the positions mentioned above, an
> individual could, by virtue of a fundamental option, remain

faithful to God independently of whether or not certain of his choices and his acts are in conformity with specific moral norms or rules. By virtue of a primordial option for charity, that individual could continue to be morally good, persevere in God's grace and attain salvation, even if certain of his specific kinds of behaviour were deliberately and gravely contrary to God's commandments as set forth by the Church. In point of fact, man does not suffer perdition only by being unfaithful to that fundamental option whereby he has made 'a free self-commitment to God.' With every freely committed mortal sin, he offends God as the giver of the law and as a result becomes guilty with regard to the entire law (cf. Jm 2: 8-11); even if he perseveres in faith, he loses 'sanctifying grace', 'charity' and 'eternal happiness.' As the Council of Trent teaches, 'the grace of justification once received is lost not only by apostasy, by which faith itself is lost, but also by any other mortal sin'.

Keeping in mind what Pope Pius XII said about encyclicals, it seems clear that in these words John Paul II intentionally adjudicated on a matter which, up to that time, was still the subject of theological debate.

BENEDICT XVI ON THE FUNDAMENTAL OPTION

I quoted John Paul II in detail, firstly so that his teaching on the connection between the fundamental option and mortal sin would be clear, and secondly, because it seems to me that Pope Benedict has chosen to talk about the fundamental option in a different way. In pars 45-46 of his Encyclical *Spe Salvi* he says,

'Our choice, which in the course of an entire life takes on a certain shape, can have a variety of forms.'

When the Holy Father talks about 'our choice, which in the course of an entire life takes on a certain shape,' surely he is describing the fundamental option even if he does not use that exact phrase. Then he goes on to talk about those who, instead of being dedicated to truth and love, are orientated to hatred because they have 'suppressed all love within themselves.' In other words, their fundamental option is evil in orientation. It is they who are destined to hell. Surely, they are a minority of people. Without naming names Benedict seems to have men like Hitler and serial killers in mind. Benedict goes on to say that one can also think of saintly people, 'who are utterly pure, completely permeated by God, and thus fully open to their neighbours.' He then observes that most of us are in between these extremes of evil and goodness.

Speaking about them Benedict says in par. 46 of *Spe Salvi,*

'For the great majority of people - we may suppose - there remains in the depths of their being *an ultimate interior openness to truth, to love, to God* (my italics). In the concrete choices of life, however, it is covered over by ever new compromises with evil - much as filth covers purity, but the thirst for purity remains and it still constantly re-emerges from all that is base and remains present in the soul. What happens to such individuals when they appear before the Judge? Will all the impurity they have amassed through life suddenly cease to matter?'

There are a number of points worth highlighting here. Firstly, the Holy Father talks about bad choices which he describes as 'compromises with evil' and the 'filth that covers purity.' However he does so without specifying whether what he has in mind is venial, grave or mortal sin. It seems to me that as an accomplished theologian, Benedict has, for unknown reasons, deliberately avoided making such distinctions. Secondly, he asserts that our compromises with evil will be fully revealed after death, in the full light of God's truth and love. That awareness will amount to a purgatorial purification, in preparation for meeting God face to face. In this connection he refers to 1 Cor 3:12-15. Some people who have undergone near death experiences say that they had such a painful awareness in the light of God's loving presence. Thirdly, it is surprising that such a knowledgeable person as Benedict does not cite Pope John Paul's references to the fundamental option. Indeed there are no footnotes in par. 46 at all.

I would suspect that any ordinary person who reads what Pope Benedict has to say about death and judgment would come to something like the following conclusion. When we face Jesus after death, instead of focusing on all the details of our lives, he will look first and foremost to see whether our hearts were basically orientated, in a conscious or unconscious way, toward Him as the fount of all truth and love. I don't think that they would conclude that a particular sin would necessarily reverse or totally cancel the significance of one's basic orientation toward God. There are many T.V. programmes which seem, implicitly, to put forward this point of view in a way that mirrors real life. For example, fictional Swedish detective Kurt Wallander, who is divorced from his wife, sleeps with a number of women and drinks to excess, has nevertheless a passion for justice, is incorruptible, shows considerable empathy and kindness to colleagues and members of the public, while disregarding dangers to his personal safety. In fact he ends up getting shot in the pursuit of his duty. Ordinary people both like and admire a flawed human being like Wallander. They may think to themselves that, while a merciful God would not approve of his promiscuity or heavy drinking, surely the Lord would judge him on the basis of the overall orientation of his life which is mostly compassionate, kind, self-sacrificing and just. This is what Jesus seems to highlight in his description of the last judgment in Mt 25:31-46. Many readers of *Spe Salvi* would conclude, with good reason I think, that this is the merciful and hopeful message that Pope Benedict is intending to convey. It is also worth mentioning that Pope Benedict seems to interpret the traditional fires of hell in symbolic rather than literal terms.

THE ATTITUDE OF POPE FRANCIS

When he addressed a Jesuit meeting in Rome in 2016, Francis spoke admiringly about Fr Bernard Haring, a well known Redemptorist moral theologian. He said, 'I think Bernard Häring was the first to start looking for a new way to help moral theology to flourish again,' Haring was a proponent of the fundamental option. It could be argued that there is indirect evidence in Francis's controversial apostolic exhortation *Amoris Laetitia* (The Joy of Love), that he inclines towards the view of Benedict XVI. For example in par. 301 he wrote,

'Hence it can no longer simply be said that all those in any 'irregular' situation are living in a state of mortal sin and are deprived of sanctifying grace. More is involved here than mere ignorance of the rule. A subject may know full well the rule, yet have great difficulty in understanding 'its inherent values,' or be in a concrete situation which does not allow him or her to act differently and decide otherwise without further sin.'

The Pope's approach seems to be similar to what moral theologians refer to as the theology of proportionalism, at the core of which is the rejection of non-negotiable, absolute moral norms. It has to said that Pope John Paul II rules out the 1960s type proportionalism in his encyclicals *Veritatis Splendor*, promulgated in 1993 (par. 75), and in *Evangelium Vitae* (The Gospel of Life), 1995 (par. 68). The possibility of admitting the divorced and remarried to the sacraments in certain, severely restricted circumstances does, at first glance, appear to be an echo of a modified proportionalism.

Speaking on Wednesday October 11th 2017 Pope Francis spoke these eschatological words in the course of a general audience,

> 'We have *already* been saved by Jesus' redemption, however, now *we await* the full manifestation of his power: when at last God will be everything to everyone (cf. 1 Cor 15:28). Nothing is more certain, in the faith of Christians, than this 'appointment', this appointment with the Lord, when he shall come. And when this day arrives, we Christians want to be like those servants who spent the night with their loins girded and their lamps burning: we must be ready for the salvation that comes; ready for the encounter. Have you thought about what that encounter with Jesus will be like, when he comes? It will be an embrace, an enormous joy, a great joy! We must live in anticipation of this encounter! . . . even if the whole world preached against hope, if it said that the future would bring only dark clouds, a Christian knows that in that same future there will be Christ's return. No one knows when this will take place, but the thought that at the end of our history there will be Merciful Jesus suffices in order to have faith and not to curse life. *Everything will be saved. Everything.*'[9]

[9] https://w2.vatican.va/content/francesco/en/audiences/2017/documents /papa-francesco_20171011_udienza-generale.html (Accessed 21/8/2018)

Judging by those words, it seems clear that Pope Francis leans towards Pope Benedict's notion of widespread salvation. Some of the Pope's critics maintain that he is a heretic because in saying that 'everything will be saved,' he was in effect denying the doctrine of hell. Notice that he said everything and not everyone will be saved. That is exactly what scripture says when it promises that there will be 'a new heaven and a new earth' (Rev 21:1) following the second coming of Jesus. At that time 'the creation itself [i.e. everything] will be liberated from its bondage to decay and brought into the freedom and glory of the children of God' (Rm 8:21).

ATTEMPTS AT A RAPPROCHEMENT

If I understand what Popes John Paul and Benedict have said about the fundamental option they seem to evaluate it in different ways. This leads to a number of possibilities.

Firstly, it could be that Pope Benedict differs from John Paul in his understanding of the fundamental option. Given the magisterial authority of their respective encyclicals, I am inclined to think on *a priori* grounds that this is unlikely. That said I was interested to see that in 1967 the German bishops published a letter in which they discussed the issue of the ordinary *magisterium* of the Church. Among other things it stated,

'The Church too in her doctrine and practice cannot always and in every case allow herself to be caught in the dilemma of either arriving at a doctrinal decision which is ultimately binding or simply being silent and leaving everything to the free opinion of the individual. In order to maintain the true and ultimate substance of faith she must, *even at the risk of error in points of detail* (my italics), give expression to doctrinal directives which have a certain degree of binding force, and yet since they are not de fide definitions, involve a certain element of the provisional even to the point of including error '

What the Pontiffs have said about the fundamental option is not *ex cathedra*. As such it may be imprecise and need further clarification.

Secondly, I wonder if what the two Popes have said about the fundamental option could be harmonised in some mutually complementary way. For example, if Pope Benedict were asked to clarify what he meant by the phrase 'compromises with evil,' perhaps he would make a distinction between mortal, grave and venial sin and describe their effects much as John Paul did, thereby tending to reconcile their two points of view.

Thirdly, it may be that Benedict's teaching represents a development of John Paul's thinking. Perhaps he deliberately avoided using John Paul's language in order to develop a more nuanced Catholic understanding of the fundamental option. Although he doesn't say so, it is quite possible that he agrees with John Paul's view that an individual mortal sin changes one's fundamental option. However, what he says in par. 46 of *Spe Salvi* seems to imply that mortal sin is relatively uncommon, maybe because of subjective and environmental factors which so often tend to diminish the culpability of what, from an objective point of view, are in themselves seriously disordered actions, or omissions. At times, John Paul seemed to share that point of view.

Christian psychiatrist Frank Lake wrote an interesting book about the Polish Pope entitled, *With Respect: A Doctor's Response to a Healing Pope.* In it he maintained that there were two sides to the Pontiff's character one liberal the other quite conservative, as his views on the fundamental option indicated. As Lake said, 'Sometimes I heard the new bell ringing out clearly, sometimes the old cracked thing.'[10] For example, we heard the 'new bell' ringing in John Paul's book, *Crossing the Threshold of Hope* when he talked about the possibility of going to hell. He said, 'Even when Jesus says of Judas, the traitor, 'It would be better for that man if he had never been born' (Mt 26:24), his words do not allude for certain to eternal damnation.'[11] Surely, this statement of John Paul overlaps with Benedict's apparently more liberal point of view.

Fourthly, Ralph Martin suggests in his book, *Will Many be Saved?* that it is possible that in *Spe Salvi* Pope Benedict may have been 'stating theological speculation and not actually teaching in an authoritative way,' i.e., about the possibility of virtually universal salvation. While that is remotely possible, it is not indicated in the text. It is significant that in the introduction to his *Jesus of Nazareth* trilogy, Benedict said explicitly, 'It goes without saying that this book is in no way an exercise of the *magisterium,* but is solely an expression of my personal search 'for the face of the Lord' (cf. Ps 27:8). Everyone is free, then to contradict me.'[12] Significantly he did not, and I suspect that he could not say that about his authoritative encyclical.

---

[10] (London: Darton, Longman & Todd, 1982), xxii.

[11] (London: Jonathan Cape, 1994), 186.

[12] *Jesus of Nazareth: From the Baptism in the Jordan to the Transfiguration* (London: Bloomsbury, 2007, xxiii-xxiv.

In 1 Jn 5:16-17 we read, 'If any one sees his brother committing what is not a mortal sin, he will ask, and God will give him life for those whose sin is not mortal. There is sin which is mortal; I do not say that one is to pray for that. All wrongdoing is sin, but there is sin which is not mortal.' Although that translation is accurate, its reference to mortal sin can be misleading, because it does not refer to our contemporary distinction between mortal and venial sin. Commenting on this verse Ray Brown said in his *An Introduction to the New Testament*, that while the inspired author urges that prayers be said that sinners might receive life because such prayers will be heard, there is an exception. He does not urge prayer for those who commit 'deadly sin' which was the relatively rare sin of apostasy or the sin against the Holy Spirit. It seems to me that when Benedict refers to 'compromise with evil' he may have this Johannine notion of sin in mind.

CONCLUSION

But when all is said and done, we will all have to face our creator in the particular and general judgments. While I hope that my understanding of what Pope Benedict has written is correct, I will be identifying with the spirituality of St Therese of Lisieux. I concur with what she said in her Act of Consecration to God's merciful love.

> 'After earth's Exile, I hope to go and enjoy You in the Fatherland, but I do not want to lay up merits for heaven. I want to work for *Your Love Alone* with the one purpose of pleasing You, consoling Your Sacred Heart, and saving souls who will love You eternally. In the evening of this life, I shall appear before You with empty hands, for I do not ask You, Lord, to count my works. All our justice is stained in Your eyes. I wish,

then, to be clothed in Your own *Justice* and to receive from Your *Love* the eternal possession of *Yourself*. I want no other *Throne*, no other *Crown* but *You*, my *Beloved*! Time is nothing in Your eyes, and a single day is like a thousand years. You can, then, in one instant prepare me to appear before You.'[13]

On another occasion Therese said to a member of her community who was worried about the prospect of having to be purified in purgatory following her particular judgment,

'You do not have enough trust. You have too much fear before the good God. I can assure you that he is grieved over this. You should not fear purgatory because of the suffering there, but should instead ask that you not deserve to go there in order to please God, who so reluctantly imposes punishment. As soon as you try to please him in everything and have an unshakable trust he purifies you every moment in his love and he lets no sin remain. And then you can be sure that you will not have to go to purgatory.'[14]

We will briefly return to the subject of the general judgement in the next chapter.

---

[13] Christopher O'Mahoney, *St Therese of Lisieux by Those Who Knew Her* (Dublin: Veritas, 1975), 48.

[14] Quoted by Michael Gaitley in *Thirty Three Days to Merciful Love* (Stockbridge: Marian Press, 2016), 79-80.

TEN

What on Earth is Heaven ?

RECENTLY I LISTENED TO A LOVELY HYMN entitled, 'I Can Only Imagine.' It was sung by Scottish singer Susan Boyle and was about the mysterious life of heaven. Some of the lyrics go as follows, 'I can only imagine what it will be like when I walk by your side. Surrounded by your glory what will my heart feel? Will I dance for you, Jesus, or in awe of you be still? Will I stand in your presence or to my knees will I fall? Will I sing hallelujah? Will I be able to speak at all? I can only imagine.' Those lyrics echo what St Paul said in 1 Cor 13:12, 'For now we see only a reflection as in a mirror; then we shall see face to face. Now I know in part; then I shall know fully, even as I am fully known.'

In this life we can only have intimations of what heaven will be like, e.g., when we experience a loving and joyful sense of belonging with other people. Speaking to some of his colleagues St Vincent de Paul spoke about such intimations of heaven when he said, 'St Paul says that whoever abides in charity has fulfilled the law....Our Lord teaches forbearance....It is a means of establishing a holy friendship among you and of living in perfect union, and in this way enabling you to make a Paradise in this world; and therefore if God gives you the grace to bear with one another, your life will be a Paradise begun.'[1] He echoed that

---

[1] SV X 478.

sentiment when he said to his Vincentian community in 1559, 'If God gives this grace to the missioners what is your opinion of the Company as a whole? Their life of love, the life of angels and the blessed, the earthly and heavenly paradise.'[2]

There is a memorable example of what St Vincent had in mind in the *Story of a Soul*, the autobiography of St Therese of Lisieux. She described a heavenly experience which she and her sister Celine shared,

> 'Those were wonderful conversations we had, every evening, upstairs in the room with a view. Our eyes were lost in distance, as we watched the pale moon rising slowly above the height of the trees. Those silvery rays she cast on a sleeping world, the stars shining bright in the blue vault above us, the fleecy clouds floating by in the evening wind - how everything conspired to turn our thoughts to heaven! How beautiful it must be if this, the obverse side of it, was so calm and clear! Perhaps it's silly of me, but that opening-up of our hearts has always reminded me of St Monica and her son at Ostia, rapt in ecstasy as they contemplated the wonderful works of the Creator. I feel as if we'd received graces belonging to the same high order as some of those bestowed on the great Saints: as the *Imitation* says, God has two ways of making himself manifest; he shows himself to some people in a blaze of light, to others under a considerable veil of symbols and figures. Well of course it was only this second kind of revelation he saw fit to give to Celine and me, but how light and transparent it seemed, this veil which hid him from our sight! How could there be room for doubt, how

---

[2] SV XII, 275.

could there be any need of faith or hope? It was love that taught us to find, here on earth, the Bridegroom we searched for. 'He came upon us alone, and greeted us with a kiss: henceforward we need fear no contemptuous looks.'[3]

Whenever we have a genuine religious experience, ecstatic joy is evoked by the awareness of the presence and love of God. That said, many important questions remain unanswered. For example, is heaven a place or a state, is it an ethereal other worldly reality or will it be here on earth? To discover reliable answers we need to have recourse to revealed truth taught by the scriptures and the *magisterium* of the Church. In a 1979 'Letter on Certain Questions Concerning Eschatology' The Sacred Congregation for the Doctrine of the Faith stated in par. 7,

'Neither Scripture nor theology provides sufficient light for a proper picture of life after death. Christians must firmly hold the two following essential points: on the one hand they must believe in the fundamental continuity, thanks to the power of the Holy Spirit, between our present life in Christ and the future life, on the other hand they must be clearly aware of the radical break between the present life and the future one, due to the fact that the economy of faith will be replaced by the economy of fullness of life: we shall be with Christ and 'we shall see God' (cf. 1 Jn 3:2), and it is in these promises and marvellous mysteries that our hope essentially consists. Our imagination may be incapable of reaching these heights, but our heart does so instinctively and completely.'

---

[3] *Autobiography of a Saint: Therese of Lisieux* (London: Harvill Press, 1958), 134.

THE PARTICULAR AND GENERAL JUDGEMENTS

We know from the Gospel of John that Jesus raised Lazarus from the dead. However, he did not have a glorified body, and after a number of years he died again. When Jesus was raised from the dead he had a glorified, immortal body. We believe, even if we don't fully understand how, that the risen body of Jesus, like that of his sinless mother was translated into heaven. That was the greatest of all miracles, the inauguration of the new creation which will become universal in Christ's coming and the resurrection of the dead. In Jn 5:28 Jesus said, 'an hour is coming when all who are in the tombs will hear his (the Son's) voice and come out.' This indicates that everyone, the righteous and the unrighteous, will experience a bodily resurrection. So St Paul declared that, 'if we have been united with him in a death like his, we will certainly also be united with him in a resurrection like his' (Rm 6:5). That is why Paul could say, 'if Christ has not been raised, then our preaching is in vain and your faith is in vain. We are even found to be misrepresenting God, because we testified about God that he raised Christ, whom he did not raise if it is true that the dead are not raised' (1 Cor 15:14-15). Speaking about the doctrine of the resurrection of the dead, par 996 of the *Catechism of the Catholic Church* rightly says, 'From the beginning, Christian faith in the resurrection has met with incomprehension and opposition. On no point does the Christian faith encounter more opposition than on the resurrection of the body. It is very commonly accepted that the life of the human person continues in a spiritual fashion after death. But how can we believe that this body, so clearly mortal, could rise to everlasting life?'

Christianity teaches that there will be two judgements, the particular judgement which will occur immediately after our

personal death, and the general judgement, which has already been
discussed in chapter nine, will follow the second coming of Jesus
and the resurrection of the dead. St John of the Cross, is reported
to have said that, 'At the evening of life, we shall be judged on our
love.' Some of those who are revived following a near death
experience tell how they were aware of a sort of particular
judgement. They saw a great orb of light which they knew to be
the presence of the God of love. In the light of that Presence they
saw their lives pass in vivid detail before them. As they beheld their
actions and omissions they could see clearly which of them was, or
was not, loving in nature. In that sense they had to judge their own
lives in the light of divine love.

Those who die in the state of grace and friendship with God, but
who are not fully purified of selfish pride, are assured of their
eternal salvation. However, they must undergo a purification to
attain the holiness needed to enter heaven. Writing in his encyclical
Spe Salvi (The Hope of Salvation), Pope Benedict XVI spoke about
purgatory in a very helpful way. He referred to the following
quote, 'Now if any one builds on the foundation with gold, silver,
precious stones, wood, hay, straw—each man's work will become
manifest; for the Day will disclose it, because it will be revealed
with fire, and the fire will test what sort of work each one has done.
If the work which any man has built on the foundation survives,
he will receive a reward. If any man's work is burned up, he will
suffer loss, though he himself will be saved, but only as through
fire' (1 Cor 3:12-15). Then Benedict went on to say, with apparent
approval, in par. 47,

> 'Some recent theologians are of the opinion that the fire which
> both burns and saves is Christ himself, the Judge and Saviour.

The encounter with him is the decisive act of judgement. Before his gaze all falsehood melts away. This encounter with him, as it burns us, transforms and frees us, allowing us to become truly ourselves. All that we build during our lives can prove to be mere straw, pure bluster, and it collapses. Yet in the pain of this encounter, when the impurity and sickness of our lives become evident to us, there lies salvation. His gaze, the touch of his heart heals us through an undeniably painful transformation 'as through fire.' . . . The pain of love becomes our salvation and our joy. It is clear that we cannot calculate the 'duration' of this transforming burning in terms of the chronological measurements of this world. The transforming 'moment' of this encounter eludes earthly time-reckoning—it is the heart's time, it is the time of 'passage' to communion with God in the Body of Christ.'

Benedict uses the word burn in a metaphorical rather than a literal way. Furthermore, he appears to believe that this purifying purgatorial experience is instant rather than prolonged in a temporal sense.

Whereas the particular judgement is a private affair, so to speak, the general judgement will be a public one. Speaking about it, Jesus said in Mt 25:31-32, 'When the Son of Man comes in his glory, and all the angels with him, then he will sit on his glorious throne. Before him will be gathered all the nations, and he will separate people one from another as a shepherd separates the sheep from the goats.' On the day of judgement there will be no hidden secrets. Jesus said, 'Nothing is covered up that will not be revealed, or hidden that will not be known. Therefore whatever you have said in the dark shall be heard in the light, and what you have

whispered in private rooms shall be proclaimed on the housetops.'
It is evident from the scriptures that although we are justified by
grace through faith in Christ's saving death and resurrection, in the
general judgement we will be assessed on the basis of what we
have done or failed to do as an expression of that faith. St Paul
wrote, 'For He will repay according to each one's deeds: but glory
and honour and peace for everyone who does good, the Jew first
and also the Greek. For God shows no partiality' (Rm 2:6, 10, 11).
In Rev 2:23 we read, 'I am He who searches hearts and minds, and
I will repay each of you according to your deeds.' Although the
scriptures say that our deeds will be under the spotlight in the
general judgement, I suspect that those sins we have confessed and
had forgiven will not appear in the book of life for the simple
reason that, God 'will tread our sins underfoot and hurl all our
iniquities into the depths of the sea' (Mic 7:19). In Heb 8:12 we read,
'I will forgive their wickedness and *will remember their sins no more.'*
The *Irish Catechism for Adults* says that 'The last judgement will
reveal that God's justice triumphs over all the injustices committed
by his creatures and that God's love is stronger than death.'[4]

HEAVEN BEFORE THE SECOND COMING
It seems to me that the scriptures and the teachings of the Church
seem to propose two images of heaven. The first is of an
otherworldly, Platonic, celestial realm which is the abode of God
and the angelic hosts. Speaking about this understanding of
heaven, St John Paul II said,

'Metaphorically speaking, heaven is understood as the
dwelling-place of God, who is thus distinguished from
human beings (cf. Ps 104:2f.; 115:16; Is 66:1). He sees and

[4] Irish Episcopal Conference (Dublin: Veritas, 2014), 178.

judges from the heights of heaven (cf. Ps 113:4-9) and comes down when he is called upon (cf. Ps 18:9, 10; 144:5). However the biblical metaphor makes it clear that God does not identify himself with heaven, nor can he be contained in it (cf. 1 Kgs 8:27); and this is true, even though in some passages of the First Book of the Maccabees 'Heaven' is simply one of God's names (1 Mc 3:18, 19, 50, 60; 4:24, 55).'[5]

Heaven is where Enoch and Elijah appeared to go following their lives on earth. When the good thief asked Jesus to remember him when he came into his kingdom, Jesus replied, 'Truly I tell you, today you will be with me in paradise' (Lk 23:43). Commenting on this verse, N. T. Wright says that 'paradise is here, as in some other Jewish writing, not the final destination but the blissful garden, the parkland of rest and tranquillity, where the dead are refreshed as they await the dawn of a new day.'[6] On another occasion Jesus said to his apostles, 'Let not your hearts be troubled. Believe in God; believe also in me. In my Father's house are many rooms. If it were not so, would I have told you that I go to prepare a place for you? And if I go and prepare a place for you, I will come again and will take you to myself, that where I am you may be also'(Jn 14:1-3). N. T. Wright has also made the interesting point that Jesus' words, 'In my Father's house are many rooms,' are often misunderstood. 'The 'dwelling-places' of this passage are best understood as safe places where those who have died may lodge and rest, like pilgrims in the Temple, not so much in the course of an onward pilgrimage within the life of a disembodied 'heaven', but while awaiting the

---

[5] One of three addresses on Heaven, Hell & Purgatory. *L'Osservatore Romano,* weekly edition in English. Heaven (28 July 1999), 7.

[6] *Surprised by Hope,* op. cit. 150.

resurrection which is still to come.'[7]   Speaking about the end times in 1 Thes 4:17-18, St Paul stated, 'we who are alive, who are left, shall be caught up together with them in the clouds to meet the Lord in the air; and so we shall always be with the Lord. Therefore comfort one another with these words.' In all these quotations heaven appears to be an otherworldly, spiritual realm.

In 1334 AD, speaking about those who have died and gone to heaven, even before the resurrection of the dead, Pope Benedict XII said in *Benedictus Deus* (On the Beatific Vision of God),

> 'Since the passion and death of the Lord Jesus Christ, these souls have seen and see the divine essence with an intuitive vision and even face to face, without the mediation of any creature by way of object of vision; rather the divine essence immediately manifests itself to them, plainly, clearly and openly, and in this vision they enjoy the divine essence. Moreover, by this vision and enjoyment the souls of those who have already died are truly blessed and have eternal life and rest. Also the souls of those who will die in the future will see the same divine essence and will enjoy it before the general judgment.'

I suspect that most Christians believe that following the resurrection of the dead on the last day those who have been saved go up to this heavenly realm where the celestial choirs pour out their thunderous praises to God and angels play ethereal, otherworldly music on their harps.[8] But that is not the orthodox Christian understanding.

---

[7] *The Resurrection of the Son of God* (Minneapolis: Augsburg Fortress , 2003), 446.

[8] Pyotr Ilyich Tchaikovsky's 'Hymn of the Cherubim' is an intimation of what that heavenly liturgy might be like.

HEAVEN AFTER THE SECOND COMING

The Bible teaches that in the end times, following the resurrection of the dead, heaven and earth will no longer be separated. They will become one when heaven will touch and transform the whole cosmos. In an important passage, the inspired author of Rev 21: 1-5 wrote,

> 'Then I saw 'a new heaven and a new earth,' for the first heaven and the first earth had passed away, and there was no longer any sea. I saw the Holy City, the new Jerusalem, coming down out of heaven from God, prepared as a bride beautifully dressed for her husband. And I heard a loud voice from the throne saying, 'Look! God's dwelling place is now among the people, and he will dwell with them. They will be his people, and God himself will be with them and be their God. 'He will wipe every tear from their eyes. There will be no more death' or mourning or crying or pain, for the old order of things has passed away.' He who was seated on the throne said, 'I am making everything new!'

What is St John saying here? In an excellent footnote, the *English Standard Version Study Bible* says that the removal of the first heaven and earth will eliminate the fatal infection of evil in the cosmic order and will give way to God's creation of a new cosmic order where sin and suffering and death will be forever banished. According to Paul the old order was in 'bondage to decay' (Rm 8:21) and 'groaning . . . in pains of childbirth until now' (Rm 8:22), awaiting the day when 'the heavens will be dissolved' and ' new heavens and a new earth in which righteousness will dwell' will be established to forever replace the old (2 Pet 3:12-13). This will represent the specific fulfilment of the prophecy given to Isaiah,

'Thus says the Lord God . . . I create new heavens and a new earth' (Is 65:13; 17). Scholars differ as to the extent and way in which the 'first heaven and the first earth' will pass away and be transformed into something new – especially as to whether this represents an entirely new creation, or whether this represents a 'renewed' creation that retains some degree of continuity with the old order. Elsewhere in the same *Study Bible,* there is an article on 'The Last Things' which says, that there will be a joining together of heaven and the renewed earth, and in company with Jesus Christ their Lord and God, the redeemed will work, play, eat, learn and worship in their resurrected, glorified bodies in the place that the Church down through the ages has always referred to as a 'new heaven and a new earth.' It will be restored to the goodness of the original creation and brought to perfection.[9]

The New Testament talks about the location of heaven. At no point do the resurrection narratives in the four Gospels say, 'Jesus has been raised, therefore we are all going to heaven' which is a rather Greek notion of a Platonic kind. The New Testament says that Christ is coming here, to join together the heavens and the Earth in an act of new creation. So it would seem that the end times are not the end of the world - they are the beginning of the real world, a restoration of the Garden of Eden. This implies that animals and plants will probably be part of the new creation and that it will be populated with people, including, hopefully, those we knew and loved during our lifetimes.

In recent years the Church has talked briefly in its official teaching about where heaven will be. For instance, the 1965 Pastoral Constitution on *the Church in the Modern World* of the Second

---

[9] 'The Last Things' in the *ESV Study Bible* (Wheaton, IL: Crossway, 2011), 2534.

Vatican Council said in par 39,

> 'We know neither the moment of the consummation of the earth and of man, *nor the way the universe will be transformed.* The form of this world, distorted by sin, is passing away and we are taught that God is preparing a new dwelling and a new earth in which righteousness dwells, whose happiness will fill and surpass all the desires of peace arising in the hearts of men. Then with death conquered the sons of God will be raised and what was sown in weakness and dishonour will put on the imperishable: charity and its works will remain and all of creation, which God made for man, will be set free from its bondage of decay.'

Par 48 of the Dogmatic Constitution *Gaudium et Spes,* (On the Church in the Modern World) says,

> 'The Church, to which we are all called in Christ Jesus, and in which we acquire sanctity through the grace of God, will attain its full perfection only in the glory of heaven, when there will come the time of the restoration of all things. At that time the human race as well as *the entire world,* which is intimately related to man and attains to its end through him, *will be perfectly re-established in Christ.'*

Not surprisingly, pars. 1042-1050 the *Catechism of the Catholic Church,* reflect and amplify the teaching of the Council. Earlier in this chapter the question was asked, will the earth be replaced or renewed as a result of Christ's second coming. Par. 1046-7 of the *Catechism of the Catholic Church* answers,

> *'The visible universe, then, is itself destined to be transformed, '*so

that the world itself, restored to its original state, facing no further obstacles, should be at the service of the just,' sharing their glorification in the risen Jesus Christ.' Par. 1060 sums up when it says, 'At the end of time, the Kingdom of God will come in its fullness. Then the just will reign with Christ forever, glorified in body and soul, and *the material universe itself will be transformed.* God will then be 'all in all' (1 Cor 15:28), in eternal life.'

THE PROSPECT OF ETERNAL LIFE

Those who believe in a heavenly life to come, are usually of the opinion, that unlike life on earth which is relatively short, it will last forever. But surely, Pope Benedict XVI is correct when he observes in par. 10 of his encyclical *Spe Salvi* (Saved in Hope), 'Perhaps many people reject the faith today simply because they do not find the prospect of eternal life attractive . . . To continue living forever – endlessly – appears more like a curse than a gift.' Nevertheless, he adds in par 11, 'we do not want to die; above all, those who love us do not want us to die. . . What do we really want? Our paradoxical attitude gives rise to a deeper question: what in fact is life? And what does eternity really mean?' He answers, 'ultimately we want only one thing – 'the blessed life' the life which is simply life, simply happiness.' In par 12 the Pontiff goes on to say, that life in heaven, albeit in a transformed universe, is outside of chronological time where one moment succeeds another twenty four seven. He explains, 'To imagine ourselves outside the temporality that imprisons us and in some way to sense that eternity is not an unending succession of days in the calendar, but something more like the supreme moment of satisfaction, in which totality embraces us and we embrace totality - this we can only attempt. It would be like plunging into the ocean of infinite love, a moment in which time - the before and after - no longer exists.' The Pope's words about being immersed in the eternal now of God's infinite love calls to mind a verse from St Paul in which he said, 'No eye has seen, no ear has heard, and no mind has imagined what God has prepared for those who love him' (1 Cor 2:9).

CONCLUSION: ESCHATOLOGY AND ECOLOGY

Because the Church believes that creation is God's gift to us and that it is due to be transformed when Jesus comes again, it is not surprising that Pope Francis encourages believers to be conscientious about caring for the natural world. His encyclical, *Laudato Si* (Praise Be to You: On the Care of our Common Home) is an ecological and eschatological reflection on how ultimate fulfilment in Christ includes the liberation and transformation of mother earth.   As he said in par. 243-244 of his encyclical,

'At the end, we will find ourselves face to face with the infinite beauty of God (cf. 1 Cor 13:12), and be able to read with admiration and happiness the mystery of the universe, which with us will share in unending plenitude. Even now we are journeying towards the Sabbath of eternity, the new Jerusalem, towards our common home in heaven. Jesus says: 'I make all things new' (Rev 21:5). Eternal life will be a shared experience of awe, in which each creature, resplendently transfigured, will take its rightful place and have something to give those poor men and women who will have been liberated once and for all. In the meantime, we come together to take charge of this home which has been entrusted to us, knowing that all the good which exists here will be taken up into the heavenly feast.'

ELEVEN

HELL AND THE POSSIBILITY
OF ETERNAL DAMNATION

I**N AN ARTICLE ENTITLED 'DEBUNKING THE MYTH OF HELL,'** journalist Carol Myer wrote in the *National Catholic Reporter*, 'I'm writing about hell because it is an unthinkable, horrible, destructive concept that can't possibly be true. I frankly can't even imagine how anyone came up with something so horrific. Could any wrong merit the terrible pain of burning in fire, while fully conscious, for a week or a year, much less eternity? What kind of a monster would inflict that on anyone? How could such cruelty and sadism be consistent with a God of love? I don't buy it for a minute.'[1] It would probably be true to say, that Myer's views would be widely shared not only by many Catholics, but by numerous members of other Christian churches. For example when a poll was carried out for the *Irish Times* in 2013 on Behavior & Attitudes, 76% said they believed in the existence of heaven, while only 46% believed in the existence of hell.[2] Nevertheless, the existence of hell is a Christian doctrine based on scripture, albeit a widely misunderstood one.

In 1936 St Faustina Kolowska wrote in par. 741 of her *Diary*, 'I, Sister Faustina, by the order of God, have visited the abysses of hell so

---

[1] Feb 3, 2011.

[2] https://www.irishcentral.com/news/irish-catholics-still-believe-in-heaven-but-not-so-much-in-hell-says-new-poll-200850691-237576921

that I might tell souls about it and testify to its existence, it is a place of great torture...The kinds of torture I saw:

- The first torture that constitutes hell is the loss of God;
- The second is perpetual remorse of conscience;
- The third is that one's condition will never change;
- The fourth is the fire that will penetrate the soul without destroying it - a terrible suffering, since it is a purely spiritual fire, lit by God's indignation;
- The fifth torture is a continual darkness and a terrible suffocating smell, and, despite the darkness, the devils and the souls of the damned see each other and all the evil, both of others and their own;
- The sixth torture is the common company of Satan;
- The seventh torture is horrible despair, hatred of God, vile words, curses, and blasphemies.

By using graphic and frightening images, Sr Faustina, like the New Testament, presents the place destined for evildoers following the general judgment in traditional imagery as a place, where people will 'weep and gnash their teeth' (Mt 13:42), or like Gehenna with its 'unquenchable fire' (Mk 9:43). All this is evident in the parable of the rich man and Lazarus, which explains that hell is a place of eternal suffering, with no possibility of return, nor of the alleviation of pain (cf. Lk 16:19-31).

Commenting on the New Testament depiction of hell St John Paul II said, 'The images of hell that Sacred Scripture presents to us must be correctly interpreted. They show the complete frustration and emptiness of life without God.'[3] Rather than being a place, hell

---

[3] General Audience of Pope John Paul II, July 28th, 1999, par 3.

indicates the state of those who freely and definitively separate themselves from God, the source of all life and joy. This is how par 1033 of the *Catechism of the Catholic Church* summarises the truths of faith on this subject:

> 'To die in mortal sin without repenting and accepting God's merciful love means remaining separated from him forever by our own free choice. This state of definitive self-exclusion from communion with God and the blessed is called 'hell'.'

Speaking about hell in par. 45 of *Spe Salvi*, Pope Benedict XVI said,

> 'There can be people who have totally destroyed their desire for truth and readiness to love, people for whom everything has become a lie, people who have lived for hatred and have suppressed all love within themselves. This is a terrifying thought, but alarming profiles of this type can be seen in certain figures of our own history. In such people all would be beyond remedy and the destruction of good would be irrevocable: this is what we mean by the word Hell.'

THE POPULATION OF HELL

The church teaches as a matter of faith that hell exists. But the question arises, is there anyone in it? Origen of Alexandria (c. 184 –c. 253) is thought to have believed in *apocatastasis*. This Greek word refers to the reconstitution, restitution, or restoration of creation to its original or primordial condition. As John Paul II said, 'according to this theory the world would be regenerated after destruction, and every creature would be saved; a theory which indirectly abolished hell.'[4] Origen's speculation led him to believe that when the new heavens and new earth came about as a result of an

---

[4] *Crossing the Threshold of Hope* (London: Jonathan Cape, 1994), 185.

intervention of God it would be universal in its efficacy. Not only would the faithful enjoy the beatific vision, lost souls and even the devil and the evil spirits could be restored. Origen's teaching on *apocatastasis* was condemned by the Council of Constantinople in 553 AD.

In an essay entitled, 'Who will be saved?' Cardinal Avery Dulles wrote, 'Catholics can be saved if they believe the Word of God as taught by the Church and if they obey the commandments. Other Christians can be saved if they submit their lives to Christ and join the community where they think he wills them to be found. Jews can be saved if they look forward in hope to the Messiah and try to ascertain whether God's promise has been fulfilled. Adherents of other religions can be saved if, with the help of grace, they sincerely seek God and strive to do his will. Even atheists can be saved if they worship God under some other name and place their lives at the service of truth and justice. God's saving grace, channelled through Christ the one Mediator, leaves no one unassisted. But that same grace brings obligations to all who receive it. They must not receive the grace of God in vain. Much will be demanded of those to whom much is given.'[5] Put briefly that is an accurate statement, but it would need to be amplified in order to be more nuanced.

The scriptures give the impression that perhaps only a minority of people will be saved. Here are a few examples.

1. In Mt 7:13-14 Jesus said, 'Enter through the narrow gate. For wide is the gate and broad is the road that leads to destruction, and many enter through it. But small is the gate and narrow the road

---

[5] *First Things* (Feb 2008). See also Ralph Martin, *Will Many Be Saved?: What Vatican II Actually Teaches and Its Implications for the New Evangelization* (Grand Rapids: Eerdmans, 2012).

that leads to life, and only a few find it.'

2.   In Mt 22:14 he added, 'For many are invited, but few are chosen.'

3.   St. Peter stated that, 'It is difficult for good people to be saved; what, then, will become of godless sinners?' (1 Pt 4:18).

In spite of these scripture texts, many of our contemporaries adopt a universalist attitude and consequently believe that the road that leads to heaven is wide and that most people take it, with the possible exception of some extraordinarily evil people. They believe this in spite of the fact that Scripture seems to indicate that many people will forfeit their salvation as a result of un-repented sin of a grave nature.

That said, St John Paul has pointed out that the Church has never spoken about the percentage of people who go to hell. 'This is a mystery' he observed, 'truly inscrutable, which embraces the holiness of God and the conscience of humans. The silence of the Church is therefore, the only appropriate position for the Christian faith.' We have already alluded to the fact that even when Jesus says of Judas, the traitor, 'It would be better for that man if he had never been born' (Mt 26:24). His words do not allude for certain to eternal damnation.'[6] If you are interested in a very well informed, balanced evaluation of the question posed in this section, see the late Avery Dulles's essay which shows that there was a virtual consensus among the Fathers of the Church and the Catholic theologians of later ages to the effect that the majority of humankind go to eternal punishment in hell. St. John Chrysostom, an outstanding doctor of the Eastern tradition, was particularly pessimistic: 'Among thousands of people there are not a hundred

---

[6] *Crossing the Threshold of Hope*, op. cit., 186.

who will arrive at their salvation, and I am not even certain of that number, so much perversity is there among the young and so much negligence among the old.'[7] Centuries later St. Thomas Aquinas (1225-1274) said that only a select few will be saved,[8] and that those who are saved will be in the minority.[9]

In more recent times, however, that view has begun to change and now eminent thinkers such as Jacques Maritain, Karl Rahner, Hans Urs van Balthasar, and Pope Benedict XIV have suggested that the majority of people may be saved. In the course of a general audience on Wednesday, 11th October 2017 Pope Francis uttered these remarkable words,

> 'If we remain united with Jesus, the cold of difficult moments does not paralyse us; and if even the whole world preached against hope, if it said that the future would bring only dark clouds, a Christian knows that in that same future there will be Christ's return. No one knows when this will take place, but the thought that at the end of our history there will be merciful Jesus suffices in order to have faith and not to curse life. Everything will be saved. Everything. We will suffer; there will be moments that give rise to anger and indignation, but the sweet and powerful memory of Christ will drive away the temptation to think that this life is a mistake.'[10]

---

[7] Quoted by Dulles op. cit.

[8] *Summa Theologica* I, Qu.23, art.7, ad 3.

[9] *Summa Theologica* I q.23, art.8, ad.3.

[10] https://w2.vatican.va/content/francesco/en/audiences/2017/documents/papa-francesco_20171011_udienza-generale.html (Accessed 11/3/2019).

Some of the Pope's critics said that his statement was heretical because he implied that everyone would be saved as Origen had once suggested. I think they misunderstood his meaning. He did not say 'everyone will be saved' but rather 'everything will be saved.' In stating this he was referring to the Church's belief about the transformation of the universe, which will finally be rid of its current 'bondage to decay' (Rm 8:21). As far as people are concerned, Francis counsels them to obey the dictates of their consciences and to rely with utter confidence on the incomprehensible mercy of the God who desires all people to be saved.

Not too long ago I experienced, for the first and only time in my life, something of the torments of hell. Instead of seeing a terrifying image, I had a profound inner sense of damnation as a total and utter separation from a sense of belonging, of relationship to God, others, creation and one's own deepest self. It was shot through with a feeling of having missed the mark and of having squandered one's potential for fulfilment. What made it feel so intolerable was the abject consciousness that all of this was definitive, irreversible and everlasting. I had a sense that in being separated from God the damned will be separated from their own humanity and will become veritable non-persons devoid of happiness, inner peace or hope. The experience was so mind-numbingly bad that I could only tolerate it for about two seconds. Afterwards, I recognised that it was the most nihilistic experience I had ever had to endure. I could appreciate why Jesus spoke about hell in such an off-putting way. In his love he didn't want anyone to go there. My glimpse into the world of the lost filled me with the conviction that not only should I strive with all my might to avoid damnation myself, but that I should also strive earnestly to help others to do the same.

TRYING TO RECONCILE SCIENTIFIC AND BIBLICAL PERSPECTIVES

As far as heaven and hell are concerned, can the perspectives of science and religion be reconciled? Currently, the standard model of the universe says that it began with the big bang, will expand indefinitely, and is subject to the law of entropy whereby it will eventually consume all its energy and turn into a cosmic graveyard. It is said that the universe started with a singularity, a beginning when all radiation and matter were compressed into an object with the possible size of a grapefruit which had almost an infinite density and temperature. When the big bang occurred some 13.5 billion years ago, at an estimated temperature of a hundred thousand million degrees centigrade, and about four thousand million times the density of water when it first began to expand. At this stage it is roughly estimated that there are more than 100 billion galaxies and that our own Milky Way is home to around 300 billion stars. Our earth is just one of countless planets orbiting one of a myriad of stars. It is estimated that it is over four and a half billion years old. Beginning around 5 billion years from now, the Sun will expand, becoming a swollen star called a red giant. By 7.5 billion years in the future, its surface will pass where earth's orbit is now. So the expanding Sun will eventually engulf, and destroy, the earth.[11]

While there are a number of theories which describe the possible ending of the universe, e.g., the big crunch, the big freeze, the big rip, eternal recurrence, it is likely that one way or the other it will come to an end. Speaking about the likely demise of the universe, Geraint Lewis, an Astrophysicist at the University of Sydney said in a lecture, that dark energy is causing the expansion of the

---

[11] 'Naked Science: Death of the Sun,' Youtube, https://topdocumentaryfilms. com/death-sun/

universe to accelerate. 'And all of the distant galaxies will one day disappear from us completely - we will never be able to see them again.' After this, in about 10 trillion years, new stars will be unable to form as the universe runs out of gas and raw material to make them. Prof Lewis added, 'As stars like the sun die, all we are left with are red dwarfs.' Red dwarf stars are about 20 percent the size of the sun and it would be difficult for any planets orbiting these stars to sustain life as they are cold and temperamental, expelling harsh solar flares packed with radiation. At this point, no life will be able to form and all that will be left will be dying stars and black holes. And Prof Lewis concluded by predicting that, 'The last star will go out, and the universe will finally go dark.'[12]

Recently I watched a science documentary entitled 'Time-lapse of the Future: A Journey to the End of Time.' Relying on what we currently know about astrophysics it tried to predict, by means of extrapolation, how and when the universe will end. The programme concluded by saying that in approximately six thousand, trillion, trillion, trillion, trillion, trillion, trillion, trillion, trillion years entropy will prevail and the universe will come to an end. The programme concluded with Prof Brian Cox saying that, 'Once the very last remnants of the very last stars have finally decayed to nothing and everything reaches the same temperature the story of the universe finally comes to an end. For the first time in its life, the universe will be permanent and unchanging. Entropy finally stops increasing, because the cosmos cannot get more disordered. Nothing happens, and it keeps not happening forever.' May I say in passing that when I heard Professor Cox's description of the dead universe I was reminded of my own intuition of hell. It was if the lost souls were alone in an utterly chaotic universe,

---

[12] Sean Martin, 'End of the World,' *The Express,* Fri, Sep 21, 2018.

devoid of any sense of relationship and where nothing happens forever. I was reminded of what St Paul says in 2 Thess 1:9, 'They will suffer the punishment of eternal destruction, away from the presence of the Lord and from the glory of his might.' Rather than referring to annihilation Paul's use of the word destruction here means ruin as a result of eternal exclusion from relationship with God in whom we find our fulfilment.

If those predictions are accurate, how can we reconcile the scientific view of the winding down of the universe and the Christian Church's notion of a new heaven and a new earth in a transformed universe? It seems to me that the God who created the universe could at some point intervene, not only by raising the dead to glorious and endless new life, as he has already raised Jesus' body, but also by calling evolution to a halt. This could be done by transcending the current laws of physics and transfiguring all matter in ways that we do not currently understand. St Gregory Palamas (1296-1359), a Greek theologian and Archbishop, endorsed this point of view when he wrote, 'The world will not lapse entirely into non-being but, like our bodies and in a manner analogous to what happens to us, it will be changed by the power of the Holy Spirit, being dissolved and transformed into something more divine.'[13]

In the first chapter I described some of Teilhard de Chardin's thinking about the elan of evolution. He believed that its goal is what St Paul referred to as the pleroma.[14] It was mentioned in Eph

---

[13] Gregory Palamas, 'Topics of Natural and Theological Science and on the Moral and Ascetic Life,' 2. *The Philokalia*, Vol IV, 346-347.

[14] *Pleroma* is a Greek word that has to do with filling or being full, or completing or being complete.

1:23, 'God placed all things under his feet and appointed him to be head over everything for the church, which is his body, the fullness of him who fills everything in every way.' Commenting on this verse, German scripture scholar Rudolph Schnackenburg says in his esteemed commentary on Ephesians: 'When the author speaks in 1:10 about 'unification' in Christ of a universe till now strife-torn, he elevates the idea to a cosmic level.'[15] Schnackenberg goes on to say: 'Wherever the linguistic key to the strange style of expression in Eph 1:23 may lie, in its thinking the conception arises that Christ as ruler penetrates every part of the universe and at the same time finds in the Church his 'fullness', the beneficent sphere of his rule.'[16] So there is a scriptural basis for what de Chardin says about the cosmic role of Christ. However, it is arguable that by interpreting the scriptural texts within his idiosyncratic world view, he may have distorted their intended meaning. For example, he saw the pleroma coming about as the result of evolutionary development when Christ would be all in all, whereas in the scriptures it seems to be the result of a sudden and decisive intervention by God.

THE PROSPECT OF COSMIC RESTORATION

While writing this book I dreamt one night that I saw a pillar resting on a circular pedestal which was made up of a number of interlocking stones. However many of them were out of place, so much so that the pillar, with all it supported, was in danger of collapse. Then I heard a voice, which I presumed was the voice of God, saying, 'I will replace the misplaced stones.' As first I presumed that God was saying that the misplaced stones would be replaced with new ones. But soon afterwards, I was given to understand that in fact the Lord would re-place the original stones

---

[15] *The Epistle to the Ephesians: A Commentary* (Edinburgh: T & T Clark, 1991), p. 60.

[16] Ibid., 60.

of the pedestal by putting them back in their proper place. When I awoke and reflected on the meaning of the dream I had a sense that the Lord was saying that a divine work of restoration was going to occur. When I prayed about the implications of this notion two interrelated inspirations came to me. Firstly, I was led to a text in Jer 17:1 where the Lord promises, 'I will restore you to health and heal your wounds.' In this fallen world, the lives of all of us are blighted, at one time or another, by spiritual, psychological and physical wounds. However, God promises those who trust in the divine undertakings that, sooner or later, they will be restored to health. The healings we witness in 'the valley of soul making' are a foretaste of the total healing of the new heavens and the new earth. Secondly, I was led to a verse in Acts 3:20-21 in which St Peter said to his Jewish audience, 'Christ appointed for you, Jesus, whom heaven must receive until the time for restoring all the things about which God spoke by the mouth of his holy prophets long ago.' I was surprised that this quotation was so obviously eschatological in nature. It asserts that the risen Jesus is in heaven from whence he will come again to 'restore all things.' When I consulted Joseph A Fitzmyer's authoritative commentary on the Acts I found that verse twenty one 'refers generically to an awaited universal cosmic restoration, often mentioned vaguely in Jewish prophetic and apocalyptic writings, e.g., as a new creation of heaven and earth (cf. Mal 3:24; Is 62:1-5; 65:17) . . . it would seem to connote a messianic restoration of everything to its pristine integrity and harmony.'[17] N.T. Wright makes much the same point in his *Surprised by Hope* when he writes,

'The New Testament, true to its Old Testament roots,

---

[17] Joseph A Fitzmyer, *The Acts of the Apostles*, vol. 31, The Anchor Yale Bible (New Haven: Yale University Press, 1998), 288-9.

regularly insists that the major, central, framing question is that of God's purpose of rescue and recreation for the whole world, the entire cosmos. The destiny of individual human beings must be understood within that context – not simply in the sense that we are only part of a much larger picture but also in the sense that part of the whole point of being saved in the present is so that we can play a vital role within that larger picture and purpose.'[18]

Amen to that. *Maranatha,* come Lord Jesus!

---

[18] (New York: Harper/Collins, 2008), 184.

TWELVE

A PERSONAL REFLECTION ON
AN APOCALYPTIC VISION

B ACK IN THE 1970'S A NUMBER OF US ENJOYED A TIME OF PRAYER and fellowship in Bundoran in County Donegal. I can remember at one point looking through a window at the Atlantic. One of the men joined me and as we both contemplated the beautiful view he said, 'Pat isn't this wonderful, we are united in mind and heart, may our union never be broken.' His words made a deep impression on me. It was true, we were united. While I shared his desire that our unity would never be fractured, I had the nagging feeling that it could be threatened by the harsh realities of a world that is often dysfunctional, cruel, and unjust.

Not long after that episode I visited a friend who had been with us in Bundoran. We chatted for a while, and began to listen to Dvorak's *New World Symphony*. At one point my friend went out to the kitchen to make a cup of coffee. As I listened to the music I experienced a three part mental vision which I have recounted in my book, *Guided by God*. In the first section I saw gentle peasants dancing joyfully in a field. I became apprehensive when suddenly I saw sinister looking soldiers marching ominously toward them, with flags waving and drums beating. 'Oh no,' I thought, 'it is always the same. Those with power always oppress the innocent and the vulnerable.'

Then the scene changed. I could see that a lot of the peasants had been killed and others had been wounded. I also noticed that, inexplicably, some of the soldiers were also dead or wounded. Spontaneously, some words from Ps 55:6 came to my mind, 'O that I had wings like a dove! I would fly away and be at rest.' Suddenly a voice seemed to speak within me, 'If you want Me to take you, I will.' I understood that God the Father was saying that, if I so wished, I could die and that he would take me to himself in heaven. I looked at the dead and the dying, and replied, 'No, I'd better stay for their sake, the dead need to be buried and the wounded need to be comforted.' Then I noticed the cross of Christ from behind. Again I heard the inner voice. It said, 'Now you have learned the meaning of merciful love, it is compassion. My Son also wanted to fly away and be at rest, but he remained for your sake.' I understood that these words referred to his anguish in Gethsemane and his resignation to God's will so that we might be saved.

Then unexpectedly the scene changed again. I could see a great orb of light coming towards the earth. I knew inwardly that it was a symbol of the glory of God. As it drew closer, the soil, rocks, and plants were bleached as they themselves became radiant with light. My body too was transfigured. By now it was rising into the air to meet the approaching orb of light. I looked back toward the earth and I could see peasants ascending, their bodies aglow with light. I saw that graves were opening and that the dead were rising in a radiant way into light, including deceased soldiers. I was puzzled by this sight. I said to the Lord, 'Why should the soldiers rise, those who oppressed the innocent and the vulnerable?' The inner voice replied, 'Because you didn't presume to judge or to condemn your oppressors, they too will be saved.'

Then the vision ended as suddenly and surprisingly as it had begun. My heart was racing, my breathing was rapid, and my spirit was exultant. At that moment my friend returned to the room and became frightened when she saw me breathing so rapidly. I think she thought I was having a fit. 'Are you all right?' she asked with anxiety. 'I have never been as right as now' I replied. 'I have just seen the resurrection of the dead and the second coming.' Then I went on to recount how the Lord had revealed a wonderful truth to me. God will never be outdone in mercy by his creatures. If believers, who have known the merciful love of God in their own lives, refuse to judge or condemn those who have hurt them, in any way, God won't judge them either. They will be saved through no merit of their own.

Ever since that wonderful experience I have reflected upon its meaning and implications many times. Firstly, it helped me to understand what the scriptures might mean when they talk about a new heaven and a new earth. In that vision I had an inkling of the fact that at the end times all matter, (especially our bodies), will be spiritualised. Not only will they be penetrated by God's glorious Spirit of light, they will be radiant with that same light. This will be made possible because as soon as the material world is brought into relationship with the fullness of the Spirit it will be transfigured like Jesus on Mount Tabor. Then the lower natural laws of the interrelated spheres of the material, biological, conscious and self conscious, will be transcended. At that time the spiritual potential hidden in them will be actualised and elevated to a higher realm which will be governed by spiritual rather than material laws.

We already have had intimations of this inchoate potential when the Holy Spirit seemed to actualise potentials which may be latent in the material world. It enabled Sts Francis of Paola (1416 – 1507) and Vincent Ferrer (1350-1419) to work remarkable miracles such as raising the bodies of dead people and animals to life. Let me give two incredible examples. Writing about St Francis, bishop Alban Butler wrote, 'After his nephew died, the boy's mother - the saint's own sister - appealed to Francis for comfort, and filled his apartment with lamentations. After the Mass and divine office had been said for the repose of his soul, St. Francis ordered the corpse to be carried from the church into his cell, where he continued praying until, to her great astonishment, the boy's life was restored and Francis presented him to his mother in perfect health.'[1] St. Antonius (1389-1459) Archbishop of Florence, a learned Dominican who was about 30 years old when Vincent died, stated that Ferrer had raised 28 persons from the dead. In her book *The Saint and the Chopped-Up Baby: The Cult of Vincent Ferrer in Medieval and Early Modern Europe*, historian Laura Smoller tells the bizarre story of how a mother killed, chopped up, and cooked parts of her own baby, only to have the child restored to life when her distraught husband brought body parts to the tomb of St Vincent who had died in Vannes in France.[2] The cessation of the usual laws of nature were also evident when St Joseph of Cupertino (1603-1663) levitated;[3] Therese Neumann (1898-1962) bore the wounds of Christ; the dead body of Catherine Labouré (1806-1876) remained

---

[1] Alban Butler, 'St. Francis Of Paola, Confessor, Founder Of The Order Of Minims,' *The Lives or the Fathers, Martyrs and Other Principal Saints*, Vol. IV, (New York: D. & J. Sadlier, & Company, 1864)

[2] (New York: Cornell University Press, 2014). See 'The Canonization Process for St Vincent Ferrer' in *Medieval Hagiography: An Anthology*, ed. Thomas Head (New York: Routledge, 2001), 795; 803.

[3] The Duke of Brunswick, patron of philosopher Gottfried Wilhelm Leibniz, said that he saw Joseph levitate twice and was so impressed that he converted from Lutheranism to Catholicism.

incorrupt; and Padre Pio bi-located.[4] As St Paul said in Rm 8:21, 'creation itself will also be set free from the bondage of corruption into the glorious freedom of God's children.'

It has also occurred to me that the Eucharist is a sign and a pledge of these possibilities. The church maintains that although the accidents remain the same, the substance of the bread and wine is changed at the consecration of the Mass. That means that God is present, body, soul and divinity under the appearance of bread and wine. As all matter is interconnected it means that God is already present in a qualified sense in the material world. It is almost as if Christ is slumbering in matter, as he slumbered in the boat on the storm tossed waters of the lake of Galilee (cf. Mk 4:38), until awakened on the last day when the divine Glory will be released in all of the natural world in an utterly transforming and glorious way. At that time there will be a cosmic *epiclesis*.[5] As we say, time and time again in prayer, 'Send forth your Spirit and they shall be created, and *You shall renew the face of the earth.*'[6]

THE CALL TO COMPASSIONATE LIVING

When afterwards I reflected on that memorable experience, it

---

[4] As F. P. Siegfried says, 'That bi-location is physically impossible, that is, contrary to all the conditions of matter at present known to us, is the practically unanimous teaching of Catholic philosophers in accordance with universal experience and natural science.' https://www.catholic.com/encyclopedia/bilocation (Accessed 10/4/2019)

[5] Epiclesis is a Greek word which refers to a liturgical invocation of the Holy Spirit for the purpose of consecrating the Eucharistic elements which result from the words of institution and is regarded as the point at which the Eucharistic bread and wine become the body and blood of Christ.

[6] This paragraph can be read as an addendum to the section entitled, 'Trying to reconcile scientific and biblical perspectives' in chapter eleven above.

struck me that it had affinities with the accounts of those who report near death experiences.[7] Secondly, I felt that it was apocalyptic in so far as it was all about the second coming of Jesus at the end of time. Thirdly, it taught me a lot about the central importance of compassion. As St Thomas Aquinas wrote, 'Compassion is heartfelt identification with another's distress, driving us to do what we can to help . . . As far as outward activity is concerned, compassion is the Christians whole rule of life.'[8] Not only is a compassionate life a preparation for meeting with God, it is also a benevolent way of living in this world.

In modern terms what exactly is compassion? Briefly put, it is empathy for those who suffer. I tried to encapsulate my understanding of that statement in the following prayer. 'Lord Jesus you told us that the teaching of the law and the prophets can be summed up in the words, 'in everything, do to others what you would have them do to you' (Mt 7:12). Grant me two gifts, the kind of love that wants what is best for others, and the empathy which not only senses in an understanding way what other people are experiencing especially those who are suffering. Enable me, by your Spirit, to have the ability to respond to them with appropriate sensitivity in emotional and practical ways. Amen'

With God's help compassionate Christians can also strive to identify with the merciful sentiments which were expressed so poignantly in the Ravensbruck prayer which was found in the concentration camp, written on a piece of paper.

---

[7] Pat Collins, C.M., 'Spirituality and Near Death Experiences,' in *Mind and Spirit: Spirituality & Psychology in Dialogue* (Dublin: Columba, 2006), 181-193.

[8] St Thomas Aquinas, *Summa Theologiae: A Concise Translation*, ed., Timothy McDermott (London: Methuen, 1991), 360.

'O Lord, remember not only the men and women of goodwill,
but also those of ill will. But do not remember all the suffering
they have inflicted upon us. Remember the fruits we bought,
thanks to this suffering: our comradeship, our loyalty, our
humility, the courage, the generosity, the greatness of heart
which has grown out of this; and, when they come to judgement, let all the fruits that we have borne be their forgiveness.
Amen.'

Some years later some Trappist priests who were living in Algeria
during a civil war opted to remain in the country in spite of very
real risks to their lives. During that time, the prior, Fr Christian de
Chergé wrote the following compassionate words to any terrorist
who might kill him.

'If it should happen one day – and it could be today – that
I become a victim of the terrorism that now seems to
encompass all the foreigners living in Algeria, I would like
my community, my church, my family, to remember that my
life was given to God and to Algeria; and that they accept that
the sole Master of all life was not a stranger to this brutal
departure. I would like, when the time comes, to have a space
of clearness that would allow me to beg forgiveness of God
and of my fellow human beings, and at the same time to
forgive with all my heart the one who will strike me down. I
could not desire such a death; it seems to me important to
state this: How could I rejoice if the Algerian people I love
were indiscriminately accused of my murder? My death,
obviously, will appear to confirm those who hastily judged
me naïve or idealistic: 'Let him tell us now what he thinks of
it!' But they should know that...for this life lost, I give

thanks to God. In this 'thank you,' which is said for every-thing in my life from now on, I certainly include you, my last-minute friend who will not have known what you are doing... I commend you to the God in whose face I see yours. And may we find each other, happy 'good thieves' in Paradise, if it please God, the Father of us both.'

In May 1996, a radical Muslim faction active in Algeria, kidnapped seven of the Trappists in the Atlas Mountains. Sometime later they were beheaded. Not surprisingly the Diocese of Algiers has initiated the process for the beatification of Christian de Chergé and his fellow monks. It is my conviction that if we humans who have been sinned against by deed or omission, are willing to overlook our right to justice in the name of unconditional compassion and mercy, God will not hold the sins of our oppressors against them on the day of judgement. As Jesus said, 'if you forgive the sins of any, they are forgiven them; if you withhold forgiveness from any, it is with-held' (Jn 20:23). While Catholics understand the words of Jesus as applying to the sacrament of reconciliation, I suspect that they have a wider Christian relevance as well.

PERSEVERANCE AND HOPE

Another aspect of the religious experience just recounted is the fact that despite all appearances to the contrary, evil does not have the last word. That word belongs to God and sooner or later it is always a word of vindication, victory and definitive blessing, if not in this life, then in the life to come which will be inaugurated by the second coming of Jesus. This was a notion that was prominent in the apocalyptic writings of Daniel who, together with his fellow Jews, had to endure the pain of exile in a foreign land. His book like all apocalyptic writing affirmed the fact that sooner or later

God would intervene to conquer evil forever. In her book, *The Spirituality of Mark*, Mitzi Minor wrote,

> 'From its Jewish roots Christianity inherited the transcendental apocalyptic faith that looked for God's presence at the end of history. Christians looked for the meaning of life in the final act of God from which all present and past events receive their explanation and significance. To seek meaning in this final act of God is to find a means of coping with the present suffering of the righteous, for an apocalyptic faith hoped for a reversal of the human condition, including vindication of the righteous soon.'[9]

It seems to me that the apocalyptic attitude described by Minor suffuses the following quote which was written by American Bishop Ken Untener (1937-2004) of Saginaw, Michigan. It was sometimes associated with St Oscar Romero (1917-1980) who was martyred in El Salvador. In 2015 it was quoted by Pope Francis.

> 'It helps, now and then, to step back and take a long view. The kingdom is not only beyond our efforts, it is even beyond our vision. We accomplish in our lifetime only a tiny fraction of the magnificent enterprise that is God's work. Nothing we do is complete, which is a way of saying that the Kingdom always lies beyond us. No statement says all that could be said. No prayer fully expresses our faith. No confession brings perfection. No pastoral visit brings wholeness. No programme accomplishes the Church's mission. No set of goals and objectives includes everything. This is what we are about. We plant the seeds that one day will grow. We water seeds already planted, knowing that they hold future

---

[9] (Louisville KN: Westminster John Knox Press, 1996), 71-72.

promise. We lay foundations that will need further development. We provide yeast that produces far beyond our
capabilities. We cannot do everything, and there is a sense of
liberation in realising that. This enables us to do something,
and to do it very well. It may be incomplete, but it is a
beginning, a step along the way, an opportunity for the
Lord's grace to enter and do the rest. We may never see the
end results, but that is the difference between the master
builder and the worker. We are workers, not master builders;
ministers, not messiahs. We are prophets of a future not our
own.'

This quotation captures a profound truth, namely that while we do
see God's grace already at work in history, it is not yet completely
in the ascendant. As Jesus' parable of the weeds and the wheat
points out, good and evil will coexist until doomsday (cf. Mt 13:
24–30). Until then there will be something incomplete and
unfinished about every aspect of the coming of the kingdom
of God. So believers need patience, forbearance, and the gift of
unwavering faith that where sin and evil abounds at present,
God's grace will more abound in the future (cf Rm 5:20). This is the
kind of hope that informed the hearts of the Maccabee brothers.
Speaking about their remarkable mother 2 Macc 7:20-23 says,
'Most admirable and worthy of everlasting remembrance was the
mother who, seeing her seven sons perish in a single day, bore it
courageously because of her hope in the Lord. Filled with a noble
spirit that stirred her womanly reason with manly emotion, she
exhorted each of them in the language of their ancestors with these
words: 'I do not know how you came to be in my womb; it was
not I who gave you breath and life, nor was it I who arranged the
elements you are made of. Therefore, since it is the Creator of the

universe who shaped the beginning of humankind and brought about the origin of everything, he, in his mercy, will give you back both breath and life, because you now disregard yourselves for the sake of his law.'

In the meantime the wheat of the kingdom grows alongside the weeds of sin and evil. In the course of a general audience Pope Benedict gave expression to this notion of incompleteness when he said,

> 'We do want this unjust world to end. We also want the world to be fundamentally changed, we want the beginning of the civilisation of love, the arrival of a world of justice and peace, without violence, without hunger. We want all this, yet how can it happen without Christ's presence? Without Christ's presence there will never be a truly just and renewed world. And even if we do so in a different way, we too can and must also say, completely and profoundly, with great urgency and amid the circumstances of our time: 'Come, Lord Jesus! Come in your way, in the ways that you know. Come wherever there is injustice and violence. Come to the refugee camps, in Darfur, in North Kivu, in so many parts of the world. Come wherever drugs prevail. Come among those wealthy people who have forgotten you, who live for themselves alone. Come wherever you are unknown. Come in your way and renew today's world. And come into our hearts, come and renew our lives, come into our hearts so that we ourselves may become the light of God, your presence. In this way let us pray with St Paul: *Maranà, thà!* 'Come, Lord Jesus!' and let us pray that Christ may truly be present in our world today and renew it.'[10]

---

[10] General Audience on Eschatology : the *Expectation of the Parousia*, St. Peter's

THANKING AND PRAISING GOD IN ALL CIRCUMSTANCES

I have a strong conviction, based on what has already been said, that we should always praise and thank God in all circumstances for everything. Reading St Paul it is evident that he saw thankful appreciation as an act of fundamental religious importance. The word to 'thank' in English is taken from the Old English meaning 'to think,' literally, 'to be mindful, to be aware of.' Appreciation as thanksgiving means that one is mindful and grateful for the natural and supernatural gifts of God. St Paul not only thanked God repeatedly himself, he said to people of faith: 'pray continually; give thanks in *all circumstances*, for this is God's will for you in Christ Jesus' (1 Thes 5:17-18). In Eph 5:20 he added, *'always* give thanks to God the Father *for everything*, in the name of our Lord Jesus Christ.'

It is obvious that we should thank and praise God for the graces and blessings of life. It is good not to take them for granted, but rather to call them to mind with gratitude. But St Paul implies that we should also thank God in spite of bad things, like illness, personal sin and persecution. He says that it is God's will that we do so. How can we thank God for the misfortunes and evil in our lives? It is not that we thank God *for* these things in themselves, but because we believe that they have been embraced by divine providence. Over the years I have come to realise that no matter what misfortunes I or others endure or what mistakes we make, they are integrated into God's saving plan for our lives. So I firmly believe that, strange as it may seem, sin, suffering, evil, injustice and vulnerability can become the birthplace of blessing. So I have come to see that to praise and thank God for everything in all circumstances has an eschatological dimension. Those prayers assert, that sooner or later, we will experience the triumph of God's reign.

It is clear that the Christian notion of divine providence, which was mentioned in chapter one, underpins this paradoxical notion of prayer. It believes that God not only has a benevolent plan for our personal and collective lives, God provides for us in internal and external ways in such a manner that we can carry out the divine plan. That said, we don't know all the details of God's purposes. They are like a tapestry which we see from behind as a jumble of coloured threads. If we could see life's events from God's point of view all would become clear. This notion is captured in a slightly updated version of the poem, 'The Tapestry,' by an unknown author.

> 'My life is but a weaving between my Lord and me; I cannot choose the colours he works steadily. Often he weaves sorrow and I in foolish pride, forget that He sees the upper, and I the underside. Not till the loom is silent and the shuttles cease to fly, shall God unroll the canvas and explain the reason why. The dark threads are as needful in the Weaver's skilful hand, as the threads of gold and silver in the pattern he has planned.'

Evidently, only God sees the true significance of providential events. But eschatological spirituality is suffused with the faith conviction that God's benevolent purposes will finally be accomplished by means of a decisive intervention by God.

THE FESTAL SHOUT OF ESCHATOLOGICAL VICTORY
We are living in the last phase of human history. The power of Satan

has been broken in principle by the death and resurrection of Jesus. As Paul wrote in Eph 1:19-20, 'God raised him (Christ) from the dead and seated him on his right in the heavenly places, far above every ruler and authority and power and dominion and above every name that is named not only in this age but in the age to come.' Knowing this to be true Paul asked in 1 Cor 15:55-57, 'Where, O death, is your victory? Where, O death, is your sting . . . thanks be to God! He gives us the victory through our Lord Jesus Christ.' Satan will be finally defeated in practice when Christ returns in glory. No wonder the commonest cry of the early Church was *maranatha* 'come Lord.' It was a sort of festal shout of praise which could be expressed in the following words, 'come Lord Jesus and we know that you will!' Nowadays, the festal shouts of those engaged in spiritual warfare anticipate the final and definitive victory of God over the powers of darkness, in human history. In 1 Thess 4:16-17, Paul tells us that in the end times, 'the Lord himself will come down from heaven, *with a loud command*, with the voice of the archangel and with the trumpet call of God, and the dead in Christ will rise first.' This great festal shout will consummate Christ's triumphant victory in a definitive way. In the meantime, Christians anticipate Christ's total victory over the powers of darkness, in their festal shouts of thanksgiving and praise. For more on this point see section four of my *Freedom From Evil Spirits: Released from Fear, Addiction & the Devil.*[11]

Surely Dianne Bergant was correct when she said, 'Apocalypticism gives people a sense of belonging to a history over which they have no control and of being secure in the thought that God, who is in control,will ultimately set things straight.'[12]

---

[11] (Dublin: Columba, 2019), 207-233.

[12] 'Apocalypticism' in *The New Dictionary of Catholic Spirituality*, ed., Michael

Conclusion

The eschatological type approach to spirituality which we have been exploring, is reflected in a special way in the Church's liturgy. Joseph Ratzinger has noted that the New Testament's apocalyptic imagery is overwhelmingly liturgical, and the Church's liturgical language is overwhelmingly apocalyptic. In his Eschatology: *Death and Eternal Life* Ratzinger wrote,

> 'The Parousia is the highest intensification and fulfilment of the Liturgy. And the Liturgy is Parousia, a Parousia-like event taking place in our midst....Every Eucharist is Parousia, the Lord's coming, and yet the Eucharist is even more truly the tensed yearning that he would reveal his hidden Glory.'[13]

Biblical scholar Margaret Barker has identified the word - *Maranatha!* - as the Church's primal Eucharistic prayer: 'This links the return of the Lord to the Eucharist.'[14] In his book, *Jesus of Nazareth: Holy Week from the Entrance into Jerusalem to the Resurrection*, Pope Benedict XIV adverted to the fact that there is a reading in the breviary for the first week of Advent which is taken from the sermons of St Bernard. It says, 'We have come to know a threefold coming of the Lord . . . The first coming *was* in the flesh and in weakness, the intermediary coming *is* in the spirit and in power, the last coming *will be* in glory and majesty.'[15]

Downey (Collegeville: The Liturgical Press, 1993), 51.

[13] (Washington: The Catholic University of America Press , 2007), 203-4.

[14] 'Parousia and Liturgy,' in *The Revelation of Jesus Christ* (Edinburgh: T&T Clark, 2000)

[15] (London: CTS, 2011), 290.

THIRTEEN

EPILOGUE

AS WAS INDICATED IN THE INTRODUCTION, this book completes a trilogy. The interrelated volumes are intended to be an apology for the supernatural dimension of the Christian life, especially the many ways in which God can and does reveal the divine presence, mysteries and purposes to us. The aim of this particular book was to answer an important question. Although we cannot know exactly when the second coming of Jesus will occur, in general terms are there any scriptural prophecies which would lead us to believe that the end time will come in the near rather than the distant future? As we have noted in earlier chapters there are a number of biblical signposts which deserve our careful attention. Let us remind ourselves of different ones which we have considered in the course of the book.

SCRIPTURAL HARBINGERS OF THE END TIMES
1] We saw in the section about amillennalism that it is the Church's belief that we have been living in the end times ever since the death, resurrection, and ascension of Jesus. The terrifying phenomena we associate with the end of the world, have recurred time and time again down through the centuries.

2] The Gospel will have been proclaimed to the whole world (Mt 24:14; Mk 13:10) even though many people will not have accepted its message (Lk 18:8). It is hard to know whether that marker event has already been fulfilled. While it is true that the Gospel has been proclaimed all over the world by missionaries, books, the mass media, etc., it could be argued that in spite of all this activity hundreds of millions of people have yet to hear anything about Jesus and his good news proclamation.

3] Conversion of the Jews (Rm 11:25-26). In earlier chapters we noted the significance of the formation of the modern state of Israel in a day and how in recent years hundreds of thousands of Jews have come to have faith in Christ as the promised Messiah. Although this development is striking and unprecedented, there are over thirteen million Jews worldwide, most of whom have not accepted Jesus as their saviour. As par. 674 of the *Catechism of the Catholic Church* says, "The glorious Messiah's coming is suspended at every moment of history until his recognition by all Israel.'

4] Apostasy (Mt 24:10-12; Lk 18:8; 2 Thess 2:3; 2 Tim 3:2-9). There is abundant evidence, especially in the Western world, that millions of people are drifting away from the Christian faith, its beliefs, morals and worship. Does this constitute a grand apostasy? Probably not. The defection mentioned in the scriptures will, in all probability, be worldwide in extent and that would not be the case at present.

5] The Final Tribulation (Rev 7:14; Mt 24: 12). The Catholic Church affirms that 'before Christ's second coming the Church must pass through a final trial that will shake the faith of many believers. The Church will enter the glory of the kingdom only through this final Passover, when she will follow her Lord in His death and resurrection' as 'the great tribulation,' based on Jesus' description of it in the Gospel. (See also Mt 24:21; Mk chapter 13 and Lk chapter 21).[1] In spite of the fact that the Church has experienced many tribulations, and currently enduring a severe one at present, clearly it is not the great tribulation mentioned in scripture.

6] The ministry of Elijah and Enoch (Mal 4:5-6; Mt 17:10-13). St Robert Bellarmine, S.J. wrote in *Antichrist*, 'On Enoch together with Elijah, many who write on the Apocalypse assert that they are going to come to oppose Antichrist, such as Bede, Richard, and Arethas. Arethas also adds that it is believed without exception by the whole Church. Moreover, John Damascene, Hippolytus the martyr, St Gregory the Great and Augustine teach the same.'[2] It is thought that they will be killed by the Antichrist for opposing him. At present there is no evidence that the two prophets have returned to earth.

7] Antichrist will be allowed to persecute the Church (Rev 13:7). Although there have been many antichrist figures down the centuries who have afflicted the Church, it is thought that THE Antichrist will appear before the end of time. He will deceive most people who will follow him and his godless messianism. There has always been evidence of the activity of the antichrist, esp. in the form of secular messianism. But one could hardly say that the powers of demonic evil have been fully unleashed upon the world, or that there is any recognisable Messiah figure in the world today.

Having considered these points, especially numbers two to four, I do not think that we have sufficient reason to think that the end times are going to occur anytime soon because many of the prophetic scriptural signs have not yet been fully fulfilled. In the

---

[1] *Catechism of the Catholic Church,* pars 675,677

[2] (Post Falls, ID: Mediatrix Press, 2015), 61.

meantime all Christians, in virtue of their baptismal identity in
Christ, are called to evangelise the nations of the world beginning
at home. As Jesus said in Mt 28:19, 'Go therefore and make disciples
of all nations, baptising them in[the name of the Father and of the
Son and of the Holy Spirit,' When that commission is finally
accomplished the ground will have been prepared for the conversion of the Jewish people *en masse* by a dramatic and sovereign
intervention of God. That will be the prelude to the second Coming
of Jesus. I was interested to see that Cardinal Schonborn, said as
much in an interview with Rev. Nicky Gumbel, the principal author
and promoter of the very popular Alpha evangelisation course. The
Viennese prelate, who like Gumbel has Jewish blood, stated that
scripture makes it clear that preaching to all the Gentiles is a
necessary pre-condition for the mass conversion of the Jews.
As a result, evangelisation is an eschatological act of primary
importance, because it will eventually make it possible for the
chosen people to enjoy the fullness of salvation.

Conclusion

On the feast of St Joseph 2019 I wondered how the Messianic Jews
understand the Second Coming of Jesus. What I found was that
one of the images they find particularly helpful is that of a Jewish
marriage. In New Testament times couples went through two
stages. The first was that of betrothal. As Prov 18:22 says, 'He who
finds a wife finds what is good and receives favour from the Lord.'
When a couple agreed to marry they took their place beneath a
marriage canopy which was symbolic of a new household being
planned, and the establishment of a binding marriage contract.
The groom would give the bride money or a valuable object such
as a ring. A cup of wine was usually shared to seal their vows.
As a result of this public ceremony, the couple entered into the

betrothal period, which typically lasted for about a year. Although they were considered to be married, the couple did not live together or engage in sexual relations. To annul the contract, the couple would have needed a religious divorce which would have had to be initiated by the husband. Matthew 1:18–25 provides an excellent example of this.

During the betrothal period, the groom had to prepare a place for his bride. Meanwhile she focused on her personal obligations such as getting her wedding garments, preparing lamps, etc. Although the bride expected her groom to come for her after about a year, she didn't know the exact day or hour. He could come earlier or later. It was the father of the groom who usually gave final approval for him to return and collect his bride. For that reason, the bride kept her oil lamps ready at all times, just in case the groom came in the night, sounding the *shofar*, i.e., the ram's horn in order to lead the bridal procession to the home he had prepared for his wife. In the Parable of the Ten Virgins (Mt 25:1–13), Jesus likened the Kingdom of Heaven to this special period of betrothal, when the groom comes for his bride, 'At midnight the cry rang out: 'Here's the bridegroom! Come out to meet him!' Then all the virgins woke up and trimmed their lamps' (Mt 25:6–7). In like manner, Jesus the royal bridegroom will come to bring his spouse the Church, i.e., the community of the saved, to his home in heaven. Jesus had this wedding imagery in mind when he said, 'Let not your hearts be troubled. Believe in God; believe also in me. In my Father's house are many rooms. If it were not so, would I have told you that I go to prepare a place for you? And if I go and prepare a place for you, I will come again and will take you to myself, that where I am you may be also' (Jn 14:1-3). That same marital imagery is referred to for the last time in Rev 21:1-2 where we read, 'Then I saw a new heaven and a new earth, for the first heaven and the first earth had passed away, and the sea was no more. And I saw the holy city, new Jerusalem, coming down out of heaven from God, prepared as a bride adorned for her husband.' When that occurs:

- Satan will be cast down to hell when Jesus comes again.
- Heaven will come to earth when Jesus comes again.
- All matter will be transformed and transfigured when Jesus comes again.
- Evil will be forever banished when Jesus comes again.
- Death will be a thing of the past when Jesus comes again.
- The redeemed will have immortal, glorified bodies when Jesus comes again.
- There will be no more sorrow, or crying when Jesus comes again.
- Suffering and pain will be a forgotten memory when Jesus comes again.
- The blessed will see God face to face when Jesus comes again.
- The joy of ultimate belonging will do away with separation from self, others, and creation when Jesus comes again.
- Cleansed of all negativity, love will suffuse all relationships when Jesus comes again.
- In the new earth thunderous worship will constantly ackowledge God's great glory when Jesus comes again.

No wonder Pope Francis has said:

'In each day of our life, we repeat that invocation which the first disciples, in their Aramaic language, expressed with the words *Marana tha*, and which we find in the last verse of the Bible, 'Come, Lord Jesus' (Rev 22:20). It is the refrain of every Christian life: in our world we need nothing other than

Christ's caress. What a grace if, in prayer, in the difficult days of this life, we hear his voice which responds and assures us: 'Behold, I am coming soon' (Rev 22:7)!'[3]

---

[3] General Audience, Wed., Oct. 11th 2017.

Recommended Bibliography

Bernard McGinn, Antichrist: *Two Thousand Years of the Human Fascination with Evil*. San Francisco: Harper, 1994.

Brian Hann Gregg, *The Historical Jesus and the Final Judgment Sayings in Q. Tubingen*: Mohr Siebeck, 2006.

Carl E. Olson, *Will Catholics Be Left Behind?* San Francisco: Ignatius, 2003.

Charles Arminjon. *The End of the Present World and the Mysteries of the Future Life*. Manchester, NH: Sophia Press, 2006.

Damon McGraw. *Apocalyptic Thought in John Henry Newman: Discerning Antichrist in Modernity*. Dissertation, University of Notre Dame 2014.

David Curry. *Rapture: The End-Times Error That Leaves the Bible Behind*. Manchester NH: Sophia Institute Press, 2004.

David Pawson. *When Jesus Returns*. London: Hodder & Stoughton, 1995.

Desmond A Birch. *Trial, Tribulation & Triumph: Before, During, and After Antichrist*. Goleta, CA: Queenship Publishing Company, 1997.

Emmett O'Regan, *Unveiling the Apocalypse: Prophecy in Catholic Tradition*. Belfast: Seraphim Press, 2011.

Frazier, Terry. *A Second Look at the Second Coming: Sorting through the Speculations*. Ben Lomond: Conciliar Press, 2005.

Henry Edward Manning. 'The Perpetual Conflict of the Vicar of Jesus Christ' in *The Temporal Power of the Vicar of Jesus Christ*. London: Burns & Lambert, 1862.

Jerry Walls, ed., *The Oxford Handbook of Eschatology*. Oxford: Oxford University Press, 2008.

John Henry Cardinal Newman. 'The Patristical Idea of Antichrist in Four Lectures' in *Discussions and Arguments on Various Subjects*. London: Pickering, 1872.

Joseph L. Iannuzzi. *Antichrist and the End Times*. Mc Kees Rocks, PA: St Andrew's Productions, 2005.
---- *The Triumph of God's Kingdom in the Millennium and End Times: A Proper Belief from the Truth in Scripture and Church Teachings*. Havertown, PA: St John the Evangelist Press, 1999.

Joseph Ratzinger, Eschatology: *Death and Eternal Life*. Washington, DC: Catholic University of America Press, 1988.

Ken Johnson. *The End-Times by the Ancient Church Fathers*. CreateSpace Independent Publishing Platform, 2016.

Michael Barber. *Coming Soon: Unlocking the Book of Revelation*. Steubenville, OH: Emmaus Road Publishing, 2007.

N. T. Wright, *History and Eschatology: Jesus and the Promise of Natural Theology*. London: SPCK, 2019.
---- *Surprised by Hope: Rethinking Heaven, the Resurrection, and the Mission of the Church*. New York: Harper/Collins, 2008.

Pat Collins. *Prophecy: Truth for Today Light for Tomorrow*. Luton: New Life, 2018.

Ralph Martin. *Is Jesus Coming Soon?* San Francisco: Ignatius, 1999.

Robert Bellarmine, S.J. *Antichrist*. Post Falls, ID: Mediatrix Press, 2016.

Roy H. Schoeman. *Salvation is From the Jews: The Role of Judaism in Salvation History from Abraham to the Second Coming*. San Francisco: Ignatius Press, 2004.

Stephen Walford. *Heralds of the Second Coming*. Tacoma WA: Angelico Press, 2013.

Timothy Paul Jones. *The Rose Guide to End-Times Prophecy*. Peabody, Mass: Rose, 2011.

Recommended Viewing

Brant Pitre. *Jesus and the End Times: the Catholic View of the Last Day*. 4 DVDs issued by Catholic Productions. (There are accompanying notes available at www.BrantPitre.com on the 'Excerpts & Outlines' link).

Brent Miller Jnr. *The Final Prophecies*. Ingenuity Films DVD 2010. ----*The Coming Convergence*. Ingenuity Films DVD 2017.

Robert Haddad. *The End Times: The Catholic View*. Arts Media Productions, 2011.

Further copies of this book can be obtained from

Goodnews Books
Upper level
St. John's Church Complex
296 Sundon Park Road
Luton, Beds. LU3 3AL

www.goodnewsbooks.co.uk
orders@goodnewsbooks.co.uk
01582 571011

other books also available by
Pat Collins C.M.

Prophecy
Guided by God
Encountering Jesus
He Has Anointed Me
Gifted and Sent
Freedom from Evil Spirits
The Gifts of the Spirit and the New Evangelisation